The
WAY OF KNOWING

This work was transcribed from the original tape recordings made of Jeshua in communion with Jayem. References by Jeshua to 'tapes' are therefore specific to the time when the recordings were made and the technology used.

If you wish to obtain the audio recordings, please visit *www.wayofmastery.com*

The
WAY OF KNOWING

Pathway of Enlightenment

The Christ Mind Trilogy; Book Three

Jeshua

Copyright © 2019 by Audio Enlightenment Press All rights reserved. No part of this publication may be reproduced, distributed, or transmitted in any form or by any means, including photocopying, recording, or other electronic or mechanical methods, without the prior written permission of the publisher, except in the case of brief quotations embodied in critical reviews and certain other non-commercial uses permitted by copyright law. Printed in the United States of America

0 1 2 3 4 5 6 7 8 9

First Printing, December 2019
ISBN 978-1-941489-43-7

WayofMastery.com
WayofMasteryBooks.com

Kindle/ePub / Audiobooks
Available on WayofMasteryBooks.com

First "AudioEnlightenmentPress.Com" Printing
December 2019

CONTENTS

Study Suggestions from Jeshua .... *i*

Foreword .... *iii*

Lesson One *1*

Lesson Two *19*

Lesson Two Question and Answer Section *38*

Lesson Three *53*

Lesson Three Question and Answer Section *69*

Lesson Four *79*

Lesson Four Question and Answer Section *95*

Lesson Five *103*

Lesson Six *119*

Lesson Six Question and Answer Section *136*

Lesson Seven *145*

Lesson Eight *169*

Lesson Nine *193*

Lesson Ten *221*

Lesson Ten Question and Answer Section *240*

Lesson Eleven *249*

Study Suggestions from Jeshua

Jeshua has also given the following specific suggestions about how to "listen" to the recordings or transcripts of these Lessons:

1. Select a separate 'Way of' notebook with a cover that has meaning for you, and a pen that you love; use them only for this work. Keep your notebook in a sacred space (such as on your altar, if you have one) wherever you live.

2. Always settle down, relax and allow the breath to flow deeply and fully before you start listening to the recordings or reading the transcripts.

3. Allow the words to simply land within you, without any effort to understand all of this information at once.

4. Notice which passages cause feelings to arise within your being.

5. Make selective notes and identify in your 'Way of' notebook those passages which touch your feeling nature.

6. Later (or on a different day) copy the passages from your notebook which elicited a strong feeling. Write them several times on a separate sheet of paper in a state of innocence and playfulness.

7. Whenever a question is asked it is useful to pause and reflect on it, before moving on.

The Way of Knowing

These Lessons were first given with the intention of each being lived with, and deeply absorbed, for at least thirty days. In reality you will find that each Lesson keeps teaching you, and taking you further into your own spiritual awakening! Listen to each recording or read the Lesson several times in different locations at different times of the day. Stay with each Lesson until you feel complete with it.

Doing the exercises as given is also very important. Many of these exercises are the same ones that were given to Jeshua by his Essene elders over 2000 years ago.

Feel free to use these suggestions as you wish, but most of all have fun with the material.

Foreword

by Jayem

The Way of Knowing is the third and final book of *The Christ Mind Trilogy,* and also the fifth of the five core texts of *The Way of Mastery Pathway.*

In the order they were first created, the five texts are *The Jeshua Letters, The Way of the Servant,* and then *The Christ Mind Trilogy,* starting with *The Way of the Heart* and *The Way of Transformation.* Each of these is equally important, for they are exactly how Jeshua meticulously set about to restore His teachings, and build the Pathway.

It is requested that the student complete *The Way of the Heart* and *The Way of Transformation* before reading and studying *The Way of Knowing.* By so doing your own studentship will have prepared, and the 'soil of the soul' will be open for receiving the revelations that He gives in this, the final core Pathway text.

Knowledge is the experience of being that which is known, not simply understanding ideas. Waking up truly and radically shatters the most fundamental illusion we all share: "I AM this separate being, this body". How untrue this is! The more we return to the knowledge of our Identity as Soul, the more what was once called 'my body' becomes 'the body.'

The body then becomes a stunning expression of Nature that gladly houses the 'living Spirit', moving, in a surrendered way, as a communication device of Love, via inspiration, creativity, and simple ecstatic celebration of Innocence.

If, that is, we take up the work of liberating it from the madness of ego, born directly from a profound, and deeply denied, fear of existing in radical freedom! This is, of course, the work of any genuine spirituality, and Jeshua's pathway is as genuinely spiritual as it can get!

Listen to His essential message in *The Way of Knowing*:

'... we come to the great culmination that you are, indeed, as I AM. That in each moment of your soul's journey you have, literally, created the worlds of your experience – just as I did when I walked upon your plane, just as I continue to do now.'

Wow!

Not much room left for victimhood or projected blame in that, is there!?

Yet see how this contradicts and corrects the two utterly essential building blocks of all egoic delusion:

~I am a victim of the world, and
~ Someone or something has done this to me!

By stark contrast to these illusions, in *The Way of Knowing*, Jeshua continues to deepen the illumination of our cosmic understanding, all while guiding us in the ways that deepen our attunement to, and flow from, our union with God. Again, every practice suggestion, and wonder question, is a call to pause, breathe, soften, and abide, letting them work in us in places our minds cannot hope to reach.

While *The Way of Knowing* is the last of *The Christ Mind Trilogy*, it is by no means the end of what He would lead us to, if we are willing and ready! Yet, IF we have truly let the teachings work on us, we will know it has given us all that we need, as we listen for the Voice within of our very soul, knowing there is awake

Foreword

within us now the choice for ceaseless unfolding. We come to realize we are not 'seeking God', but unfolding IN God, whom we never left!

Just this is the joy of Life, of Creation, of Existence. And we come to know this the more we are BE-ing this!

I feel to address a great temptation here. It is one that we find with so many students and teachers of *A Course In Miracles*, and *The Way of Mastery Pathway*. Indeed, it's a pretty universal temptation.

What is it? The temptation to believe that 'now I have got it'!

In *A Course In Miracles*, He begins to wean us from that temptation by reminding us He has delivered us into the hands of the 'internal teacher' (the Holy Spirit), who will guide us now. It is so easy for the mind to conclude 'I am finished', when in fact, He is saying: 'This is not an end, it is a beginning. You are now prepared for the Journey. Surrender, and be taught.'

In *The Way of Knowing*, He does the same. You will notice that He says: 'you now have all that you need to begin or deepen your journey.'

Again, the ego will tempt us sorely to take this to mean: 'I am done, this is all I need', and at this crucial point, we can become attached to this idea, rather than surrendering into an even greater devotion in studentship.

What He clearly is teaching us, rather, is to be surrendered in every moment, to leave our conditioned minds behind, and to rest in ever deeper trust, discovering increasingly what it means to be moved from and within Spirit.

The Way of Knowing

Listen, then, and drink in His words from the final Lesson of *The Way of Knowing*:

'The secret then, as I have shared with you many times, is to PRACTICE seeking first the kingdom. NEVER let a day go by in which you fail to ponder the great mystery of God's Presence.

Never let a morning go by that you fail to begin your day, except in this way:

Surrender all thought of what you know and what you have believed. Rest in gratitude to the One Who has birthed you.

Ask only to be revealed for you greater Truth, greater wisdom, greater capacity to know and extend perfect Love, perfect trust, and perfect peace.'

I like to say that if anyone sticks with *The Way of Mastery* teachings this far, there is no hope they will ever leave the Cosmic Hotel California again. Never again tempted by mere delusions. No more able to fool themselves into thinking Separation ever occurred, nor to deny the shimmering beauty of all things, the exquisite orchestration of Love, as it simply works to reveal more of itself in us, as us, and for all beings.
Eternal gratitude to our teacher and Way Shower, Jeshua ben Joseph!

Blessings,

Jayem

December 2019

Lesson One

Lesson One

Now, we begin.

And indeed, once again, greetings unto you, beloved and holy friends. We come forth to abide with you now as we initiate the third and final year of this *formal information* that we have sought to share with you. This information will, in time to come, be shared with millions. We have chosen to entitle this year's lessons *The Way of Knowing*.

What, then, requires *True Knowledge*? What, then, is required for True Knowledge to exist? How does one live—in whatever dimension of Creation—when they abide in True Knowing? Beloved friends, that which is required for *True Knowledge* to pervade the whole of one's consciousness is simply this: *Not for one moment* have you *ever* lived life. Rather, in Truth, and in Reality, Life, which is but Love streaming forth from the Source of all Creation, has *sought* to live *as you*. Never at any time has there, in Truth, been a false self. Never has there been a time in which something called the ego has existed.

You have heard us say unto you many times that what is true about you is true always, and that you remain as you are created to be—the Thought of Perfect Love in form. You emanate from the Mind of the Creator as a wave emanates from the ocean. The great secret of your human existence, indeed the great secret of the many journeys you have taken, is that they have existed *nowhere* save *within* the movie screen of your own mind.

Does this mean that your dreams have had no effect? Within the dream itself, as long as you choose to be identified with it, you *will* experience the effects of the choices which you have made. And yet, now, as the heart has touched purification and as you have truly been willing to allow transformation to occur, all that matters and must be remembered is that *you*, as you *thought* yourself to be, has never truly existed. It has been a smoke screen. It has been a chimera. It has been illusion.

Knowledge, then, consists of the crystal-clear awareness that while Creation streams forth from the Mind of God, *you* cannot find the place that a separate self began. And you have absolutely no knowledge of where your end will be found. In Truth, *you* do not know what is going to unfold in the very next moment of your experience. This can only mean, since you *do* have a next moment, that *something else is living you.*

In the beginning of the journey, there must be *desire*, for no one can come unto the Father without it. For just as you used the energy of desire to dream the dream of separation that closed your heart, that set you on a thousand useless journeys, propelled and compelled by fear, by judgment, by doubt — likewise, desire has been necessary for you to be willing to face your illusions, to look more deeply at your judgments, and to see that they can have no value save that which you extend unto them. It has, indeed, required desire for you to *want* to awaken.

As you have used the power of *intention* to continually etch into the mind the beliefs and perceptions that are the very foundation of the dream of separation, so, too, have you learned to use intention through time, which is your creation, in order to awaken from time and from fear.

Just as you once used the power of *allowing* to give permission to the creations held within your mind to seemingly — apparently — take form in front of your eyes, and allowed their "reality" to become so deeply entrenched that, literally, worlds have been birthed from it, so, too, have you needed to use allowance in the process of transformation, *allowing* yourself to feel what you did not want to feel before, to see differently what you had once insisted could only be seen in a certain way.

Lesson One

Allowing has been the very field from which all forgiveness you have learned has sprung forth. Allowing has been the most central of keys in the process of your healing and awakening. For when you truly begin to touch upon the power of *genuine allowing*, you begin to taste the first levels of *true freedom*. You have learned that just as you have allowed new beginnings to occur, you have also discovered that you have the power to allow endings to occur within the field of phenomena you call "the world."

And yet, I say unto you, *surrender* is the completion of the Keys to the Kingdom. Just as once you had need of surrendering to your illusions in order to identify the fundamental energy of your being *with* your illusions, just as you have had to live in surrender to even allow allowance, just as you have learned to rest in surrender even to allow intention, just as you have learned to rest in surrender even to allow desire to be made new within you, as you enter *The Way of Knowing*, the *final surrender* is entered — that surrender which is beyond the comprehension of all the languages and theologies of your world, beyond all that can be spoken or uttered, yet not what can be *known, felt, realized, and lived*!

For in surrender you look upon a perfectly harmless world, whether it seems to be outside of the body or within the body-mind, itself. You look upon the comings and goings of the world and you find that all things are, of themselves, perfectly empty. You look within and discover that no longer need you *obstruct*, from the conscious mind, from your awareness, what the body-mind has experienced from the moment of its conception. No longer is there an *obstruction* to the *flow of experience*. No longer is there a *self seeking God*. And where and when that self has been surrendered, the mind awakens to the simple Reality that there is *only* God. And *you are* That One.

Yes—as you seek to find words to communicate to yourself, or perhaps to another, the great wonder, the great mystery, the great Truth, the great simplicity of awakening into True Knowing—you will strive to find a way to communicate, as I have tried to find ways to communicate with you. You will seek to communicate to your brothers and sisters that there is only God, and yet . . . and yet . . . there is the power of the mind to perceive yourself as the Created—which in Truth, you are. For *God gives rise to God, looking back upon Himself.* Mystery of pure content gives rise to temporary form in order that Pure Mystery might be apprehended.

You are, then, the very process whereby That One who alone is without a second creates the temporary form through which That One apprehends and knows Itself. You are That One that is the perfect *effect* of Mystery, that would pour forth of Itself and make visible what was invisible; to birth through time and form that which cannot be contained within it. For Love is unfathomable. You cannot control it. Love is vast beyond all measure. You cannot contain it. Love cannot be possessed. It can only be allowed.

Therefore, indeed, beloved friends, the very Keys whereby once you used the power of your own mind to create the illusion of a separate self, are the very Keys utilized by your own mind to awaken you to the Truth that you have never been, that there is only and always *this* mysterious moment. And all things have been birthed from Perfect Mystery.

The Awakened Mind—awakened from false arrogance—looks upon all things and says,

> *I am That One.*

Lesson One

And yet, no trace of separation or duality exists, for you are not apart from all things that are arising: the wind that blows through the trees, the wisps of a cold winter rain, the warmth of the sun upon the skin of the body, the embrace of a lover, the laughter of a child. The Awakened Mind that abides in Perfect Knowing no longer *obstructs* perception, feeling, the flow of thought, the flow of experience. It no longer looks to see how it can make things *different* than they are. It looks only, and lives from, what it most truly wants: simply to abide in its own nature and to allow Life to flow from that nature, dancing in the infinite myriad displays of form.

What, then, is required for True Knowledge to exist? What is indeed required to abide in *The Way of Knowing*? To *fully accept* that *not one trace of your seeking* has ever brought you closer to Reality; that *not one modality* has ever held the *power* to bring you closer to God; that *never* could it have ever been truly possible for you to make progress toward the Consciousness of God. For all the while, you have been the One you are seeking, *pretending* to be a seeker. And for what reason, for what reason have you entertained the thought of separation?

The reason is simply this: *to do it*. For the Mind of God does not deny *any* possibility, for It sees nothing that can obstruct the purity of Its own nature. And forever the Father abides within Himself—infinite, vast, radiant, silent—the Infinite Field of Pure Knowledge, Pure Intelligence, out of which *all* things, and *all* possibilities arise. This is why I once said unto you,

You have never looked upon another, for you see only *your Self.*

You are free to judge yourself by judging your brother and, thereby, create a form of experience. But even that form of experience is *only* the Perfect Reality of God. And *That* is what you are!

What, then, requires True Knowledge? God does. And from the very moment that you first had the thought,

I want God,

even that thought has appeared within the field of what you believe is your limited awareness as a limited body-mind, racked by fear and doubt and guilt and all of the rest—all of it is illusion. That thought of wanting God, the moment in which your journey home began, *that thought* is the presence of God awakening Itself to that which has never been lost.

God is what requires True Knowledge. The thirst that you have felt for God is God's thirst for Herself. You are literally the Field of Awareness of God in which God has awareness of Himself, because you are the Power of God, and *only* by that Power have you ever been able to be aware of *something* that has appeared to be *other* than God, for *even fear rests in Love.*

Even fear, contraction, and the dream of separation *require Love,* for Love *allows* all things, *trusts* all things, *embraces* all things, and therefore *transcends* all things. And in your own, what you might still wish to perceive to be your "own experience," as though it were separate and apart from your brothers and sisters, as though it were separate and apart from the twinkling of the stars, and the dance of the sunlight upon the water, and the thought in the brilliant mind of a scientist, and the cry of a newborn child—even if you wish, yet, to maintain that you have something called "private experience," that private experience has required the presence of God. Every thought you have ever held has existed only because *Love has allowed it!*

Have you suffered, then, because God has chosen it? Not at all. For in Truth—and please listen carefully—*suffering does not exist.* Only the Reality of Love can exist. And you are That One

Lesson One

with the *power* to be awakened to your true nature — right now, right here! Indeed, only when you have given up attachment to the modalities, the meditations, the prayers, the theologies, the textbooks, only when *you* have given up attachment to all form and merely make the decision to abide in the Simple Knowledge that you are That One, *only then* does Knowledge permeate your awareness.

If there was something you had to *do* to *get* to God, then God is apart from where you are. Yet it is the very Love of Pure Consciousness that gives you the power to perceive that there is something you must do to get to God — and therefore, God is always present. If there was truly some form of meditation that could enlighten you, it would mean that *you* were *truly* apart from God at some point. But it is not possible for That One to be separate from Itself. Allow, then, the mind to rest in the simplicity that what is true has been true always, and that where you abide you are merely the manifestation of That One showing up as a man or a woman.

In True Knowledge, in *genuine True Knowledge*, which exists NOW HERE, and cannot be gotten tomorrow, there is only the pure simplicity of the moment which is arising, looked upon with perfect innocence. In True Knowledge there is perfect peace. In True Knowledge one merely abides awake, witnessing the play and display of phenomena which are, indeed, arising only within that one Mind that the Sonship is.

I have said often to you that you cannot truly make a wrong turn, and no one has ever made a wrong turn in their journey. How could this be possible in the Field of Pure Love that is God? And only Love is Real. You have merely allowed yourself — as God — to formulate shapes of experience merely to experience it. Every tear that you have cried, every loss that you have felt is yet only God choosing to have the experience. And you have remained eternally free in each moment to choose again. And indeed, you will choose again without end. For there is not a "time" that God will cease to be. For if God could cease to be, then God is not God, for there would need to be a field of energy in which non-being could exist.

The Mind that is Awakened serves only the Holy Spirit, and the Holy Spirit is merely Right-mindedness. And what is Right-mindedness if not True Knowledge?

The Way of Knowing, then, is a way of unobstructed feeling, unobstructed allowance, not only of what is around you, but what is *arising* from within you. The work that I do through this, my beloved brother, is not done because someone else is requiring me to do it. It arises within the Field of the Mind of God that *is* the essence of all that I am as Christ. It arises, is witnessed and allowed by me. And therefore, the work is done. This is no different than what you experience in your moment-to-moment experience. When you watch a raindrop fall and touch the window through which you look, you have utilized, and indeed are, the presence of the Power of Awareness that is no different than that which pervades me and through which this communication work is manifested. All that is taking place in all attempts to awaken the Sonship is that That One is speaking to Itself. It speaks of awakening because another aspect of Itself, another wave from the ocean, is yet *pretending* that it has *truly* caused itself to lose awareness.

Look, then, around you, beloved friends. For once I asked you to consider that you do not know what a single thing is, or is for. I did this because you *believed* that you were a separate self, and that your judgments and perceptions and definitions of things had a reality *outside* of your mind. And therefore, I asked of you,

Lesson One

Look around in perfect humility, for you do not know what a single thing is, or is for.

For if you look upon a brother or sister and see them as separate from yourself, something or someone from which something can be acquired for you to gain in your journey, you have truly not known what your brother or sister is for. This is the only thing that your brother or sister *can* be for: *to be that which God looks upon and sees only Himself.* A brother or sister is in the field of awareness you have learned to call your own for one reason: *to be loved, to be celebrated, to be joined with to create and extend the good, the holy, and the beautiful.*

Does this mean that if you look upon another that they *ought* to get it? Not at all. For That One that you are, manifesting through them, may very well choose, in its infinite, perfect freedom, to remain wholly insane. And so what? Nothing can prevent you from looking with Love and allowing the play and display of form to continue its dance—birth and death, joining and distancing, creating and dissolution. All things that can be experienced must finally be allowed to flow without obstruction within your mind. Birth gives rise to death, and death gives rise to birth in a ceaseless display—not of something struggling *for* life, but *as* Life, Itself.

The Reality of all that you are remains utterly changeless and pure. You are as the sky through which all clouds dance and play. Your literal moment-to-moment experience, even in the moment when you think you are only a separate self that's going to go bankrupt tomorrow because of decisions made yesterday, even *that* can be allowed, can be trusted, can be appreciated, can be witnessed from the spaciousness of the sky that can embrace each cloud from a place of Perfect Knowing.

There can be no greater joy than to arrive in each moment with nothing to be acquired, nothing to be accomplished, and *nothing to be resisted*. When resistance has been released, through the simple choice to release it, you will discover and know that all along, in Reality, there has only been God.

How, then, does one live as they abide in True Knowledge? One could simply answer,

Any way they want to.

For in unobstructed Life, That One is allowed to *in*form your choices. There is no longer anything you believe you need, nothing you believe will add something to you. For who by taking thought, who by taking action, who by belief in theology, has ever added even one inch to their stature? For though the body arises and passes away, as a brief cloud of illusion in the Field of Creation, you remain unobstructed and vast. And how can eternity be added unto? You are Pure Awareness. And nothing you have ever done has increased you, just as nothing you have ever done has taken anything away.

Each moment, then, is perfectly pristine and honest and innocent. Each moment, embraced and allowed without obstruction, *is* the literal and present state of Heaven. This is why I once said,

Heaven is spread across the face of the Earth, yet mankind sees it not.

And yet, it requires Heaven to *choose* to see something else. This is the slippery point upon which our final year together rests. And it is slippery only because *it requires no effort*. You cannot help but be the One showing up as the dance of a temporary play of energy that *appears* to be separate from all other plays of energy. And yet, the Sonship is One. Every tree, every drop of

Lesson One

rain, every molecule, every thought, every non-thought — these things are the Sonship. Is it not time to awaken beyond a particular language that speaks only to *humanity*?

Remember that your suffering has come only from the illusion that you are a separate body-mind subject to the ravages of time, the insecurities of the world, surely to become a victim of death. The whole time, in Reality, you are the *power* by which you chose that belief! Does this mean that you can merely say,

> *I am awake now and I don't need to feel that feeling that's coming up?*

Not at all! For Love does not resist *anything*. Love *embraces* all things. Love *desires* all things. Love *awakens* to the Truth that only God is, and God would embrace the totality of His Creation *through* you, *as* you, *in* you, *for* you and for Himself! For there is no difference between God and you. *You are That One*.

How, then, does an Awakened One live? I gave you the answer earlier: any way that that Awakened One wants to! And here now, please understand, we come to the *essence* of what we'll be doing this year. For no longer will we live in questions about what we *ought* to do. No longer will I ask you to live in questions of what went wrong, but rather, in the purity of the power of the one question that God dwells in constantly:

WHAT DO I WANT?

For here, in perfect surrender, is the mind returned to pure desire — not the desire to gain for a separate self, but that which expresses the totality of God.

What do I want?

is the question that God asks Himself *as you.*

Yes, it does mean you are perfectly free to enjoy the field of desire. Are you capable of knowing what you truly want? Absolutely, once you decide that you are not what you once believed you were. This requires only the decision to recognize that nothing can exist save God, and that, therefore, you are That One. You are whole and free—NOW!

I have often hinted to you that the totality of my life was *my journey* back to God. I chose it freely, not because I was separate from God, but because I had already awakened to the Truth that,

What could possibly exist except the Love of God?

And I chose, then, to look upon the body-mind and live only in the question,

What do I want?

And one thing I chose was to demonstrate the *unreality* of death.

What will *you* choose to demonstrate? For see not in my demonstration something grand and beyond you, but rather, see that everything you demonstrate is *equal to* that same power. For it *flows* from that power, it *abides* in that power, it *manifests* that power, it *is* the Living Breath and Reality of God!

And therefore, as we continue through this year, we will begin to focus attention in the perfect freedom of exploring what is wanted. For the Awakened Mind sees that in truly living in divine selfishness, you cannot help but dance perfectly with your brother or sister, regardless of how they are choosing to respond to you. It is impossible to be separate one from another.

Lesson One

It is impossible to cause another suffering. It is impossible not to be One with the one before you. There is only the dance and the play of Creation. There is only the celebration of God's Eternal Reality. There is only the recognition that God is Joy and not depression. All depression stems from resistance, the obstruction of the flow of awareness, the attempt to limit the unlimited.

The mind that allows all things, trusts all things, embraces all things — *is* all things. And yet, though, you will seem to live, yet you will not live. But That One alone lives as you. You are free. You are vast. You are without birth and without death. You are as I am. You are the Awakened One, the Anointed, the Messiah. You are the gentle touch of Love in a temporary illusion, attempting to be other than Love. And why not? It's all a simple game, a simple play — an innocent illusion.

And therefore, indeed, we will end this hour with this one question that we would ask you to live within between now and the time we next communicate with you:

Beloved friend, O Holy One: WHAT DO YOU WANT?

And is that wanting generated by the freedom of Love or by the ridiculous creation of a useless fear? Want only from freedom and you will have your desire.

And with that, beloved friends, peace be unto you always. We are most certainly going to enjoy this year with you. Go, then, in peace.

Amen.

The Way of Knowing

PERSONAL NOTES

Lesson One

PERSONAL NOTES

The Way of Knowing

PERSONAL NOTES

Lesson Two

Lesson Two

Now, we begin.

And indeed, once again, greetings unto you, beloved and holy friends. As always, it is with great joy that we come forth to abide with you in this hour and in this manner. For the forms of communication are virtually unlimited. Communication requires only the willingness of any two minds to *join in communion*. Communion requires the willingness to rescind one's investment in being right. Rescinding one's investment in being right requires recognition that either mind does not know what a single thing *is* or is *for*.

For in that journey, which began in *The Way of the Heart*, and continued with *The Way of Transformation*, and begins to culminate in *The Way of Knowing*, surely, you have heard me say to you, countless times and in countless ways, to awaken in remembrance absolutely requires that you choose to want—above all things—to *think with the Mind of God*. And to think with the Mind of God requires that you be *taught anew*. To be taught implies a *willingness to learn*. And a willingness to learn implies that one is willing to create a *space of emptiness within* that can be filled with a new substance, a new elixir, a new alchemical substance, if you will.

Therefore, that pathway that brings the soul into perfect remembrance requires the cultivation of the **Keys to the Kingdom: Desire, Intention, Allowance, Surrender**. The most essential of those Keys, again, is *Allowance*. For there is no one listening to these words who has not already cultivated at least a sufficient Desire. It may not be one hundred percent perfected, but the Desire has been there. For no one would come into my presence, no one would come into communication with that group of beings—masters, teachers, friends . . . By the way, we choose as a group to be known as simply "The Lineage," for which I remain the primary spokesman through this, my beloved brother, but there are many forms of our communication with mankind . . . No one would come into this presence who has not *already desired* healing, awakening, and remembrance.

Intention is the only place that you can begin to correctly use the *will* that was originally your Creator's Gift to you. For the correct use of will, or clear Intention, is to bring forth the good, the holy, and the beautiful. And any mind that reflects upon its experience and has come to see that, often, fear has been in the driver's seat more than Love, will rightfully use Intention to ask for help in gaining correction of the mind, that itself, that mind, that soul, might again come into alignment with the Will of God.

Coming into alignment with the Will of God is not an act of subservience, although it feels as such to the insane ego. But to the pure of heart, to the meek who shall inherit the Earth, to those who recognize their insanity and want a transformation to perfect sanity, aligning with the Will of God through clear Intention is to seek for that which is one's greatest good. It is not a loss at all. It is *perfect remembrance*. Coming into that alignment, then, is like one who gives up one of your golden coins to receive ten million golden coins. It is as though one would give up a rag doll in order to step into a true love relationship of flesh and bone and emotion and passion. It is as one who would give up the hope or wish for a drink of water and go to the faucet, if you will, and fill the cup with living fluids.

Understand, then, that Intention, when it is focused wholly on *wanting only God*, can never take anything from you that you truly want. And it will come to replace for you that which you've always wanted, have known in the ancient past, and are calling back to you now.

Lesson Two

Desire, Intention, Allowance... *Allowance*. Oh, indeed, beloved friends, and there are many of you that have come to taste the Truth of what I am to say. Allowance is the greatest of Keys to the Kingdom. For Allowance requires a rescinding—slowly, patiently at times, painfully at times—a rescinding of every perception you have ever held of everyone and everything. It is the descent into complete recognition of your ignorance, a complete recognition of your joy-filled dependence on the corrective power of the Holy Spirit.

Allowance is the greatest of Keys to the Kingdom. This requires cultivation *in time*. And when there has been the Desire for healing and awakening, rest assured, that already your Father, through the Holy Spirit, is working to reshape every moment of your experience—*every single moment*—so that the correct teachers, the correct lessons, the correct books, [laughs] even the correct weather, can come to force you to look at your edges of *unhappiness*, your edges of *judgment*, your edges of *insecurity*, your edges of *fear-based definitions* of what Love is, what it should look like, and what its effects should be. In other words, the entire world that you have made in error *must* be brought to the surface of the mind for correction.

Allowance is sweet above the taste of honey. For Allowance is that realm in which miracles can finally begin to occur. And what is a miracle? It is not really a change at all. It is merely the recognition of what has always been—that there is a Love, a Power, that would live through you, that would guide you in all things; that you need not be the captain of the ship, you need only be willing to take the cruise.

These three Keys, which are *active* in a sense, that is, they are experienced in time, they bring up questionings, they require some resolve and commitment and faith, culminate in *Surrender*. But this culmination is not something that you do for yourself. Rather, when the seed has been well planted, when the ground has been tilled and cultivated, when the wise farmer has made sure that the weather conditions, the watering conditions, and everything, are just right so that the seed can be well nurtured, Surrender is much like the petals which emerge *in their own time*. Here the farmer can do nothing but wait for Grace to descend.

He may not see that the petals are emerging as the result of *all* things that have gone forth before: in the selection of the seeds, in the waiting for the perfect time to plant, in each day's cultivation and weeding of the garden. *Choosing* to enter times of prayer, in other words. *Choosing* to see where fear has made a home in the mind and surrendering it to the Holy Spirit. *Cultivating* turning over each decision, day by day, moment by moment. He may not see the causal connection. He will only see and witness the emerging of the petals. That emerging has been called, in some cultures, "extraordinary" gifts, such as clairvoyance, clairaudience, the ability to leave the body, the experience of communicating with discarnate beings, such as myself, the ability to see and read the soul of another.

But more important than all of these is *Peace*. Peace is the culmination of the spiritual journey. It becomes the *field* in which one has entered the Kingdom and now journeys within it in perfect freedom—a freedom that cannot be understood by the minds of mankind that still live in fear, doubt, separation, and even the most subtle traces of egoism. *Peace is the goal*. But Peace is not a passivity. It is really the *seat of creative power*. For you were created to create the *good*, the *holy*, and the *beautiful*.

For a while, you learn to create something else. And yet, that creation has occurred nowhere, save within the mind. It is merely a chimera or an illusion. But as you cultivated the power to create illusion, so, too, does the journey to God require purification—that process whereby you surrender your will, the egoic mind, over to correction by the Holy Spirit.

This journey will take you into what this, my beloved brother, calls "the essence of what you do not know you do not know." That is what makes it *unconscious*. For you have used the power of the mind to push down out of yourself your fears, where they actually gain power but you do not need to confront them directly. Denial or suppression, as they speak of it in your psychological language, is the very root of the creation of the ego. And that which has been hidden *must be made known*. And in its being made known, *purification* can occur.

Rest assured, then, as I've shared with you many times: Give thanks unto the saviors that are sent unto you. They come in many guises and forms. Some of you would look upon me as your savior. And in the sense that I am sent unto you as a teacher, I am. But it is only the *teaching* that saves you, not me. Your saviors will often, and more often, show up unto you as those who evoke within you your deepest reactions, your vehement judgment, your *certainty* that *you* are *right*! When these things occur and your peace is disturbed, your greatest reactivity has been triggered, your greatest emotionality is triggered, *there* is the *edge* that calls for your attention! For remember always, that nothing can come to you unless you have called it from within yourself in order to grow more deeply in forgiveness, in wisdom, in Love, and in the Power of Christ.

As purification begins to touch most fundamental or most radical levels, the *sweetness of Peace* begins to be remembered—faintly at first, and then more and more, and more and more. One has a realization. Remember the whole journey is merely one with no distance to it at all to a goal that's never changed—it is just a change of mind, a remembrance. Realization, then, may be the recognition that,

> Oh, I used to think this way, but now I see the emptiness of such silly things.

That quickly [snaps fingers], that fast—it's over, it's gone. Where did the illusion go? It got erased by the cosmic eraser on the end of the pencil held by the Holy Spirit, because of your *Desire*, your *Intention*, your *Allowance*, and your *cultivation* of all of those tools that support you to choose again, to want only Love.

Grace purifies the mind. And Grace is a direct gift of your Father. It is that energy or Power of Love that descends into a mind and heart that prepares a place for it. You could say that your greatest preparation is to admit that you do not know what anything is for. That if you're feeling emotions, if you're feeling like you want to run, if you feel like you want to avoid taking responsibility for something that's been dropped in your lap, rest assured, *right there is your edge*. There is the place you need to *turn back* and *embrace*.

And in the end, once the journey has begun, the end *is* perfectly certain. Peace is the perfect goal. But there are few, still, who truly understand what Peace is. It is not the *avoidance* of pain. It is not the *avoidance* of responsibility. It is the *doorway* to the *greatest* of responsibilities in which the mind, the heart, the soul, and even the body, while it lasts, has been so purified of dissonance, it has become so aligned with the Will of God, that it looks upon all things with the Compassion of Christ. Such a one walks this world of yours *unknown* by those around him or her. That one serves only the Voice of the Holy Spirit. It is not the least bit concerned with others' reactivity. For the only goal of the Awakened Christ—and Peace and Christ Consciousness are one and the same—is to be an agent through which the

Lesson Two

Power of Grace works to transform illusion. That Mind serves the Atonement. That Mind may not be understood by others, but how can the *insane* understand the *sane*?

Indeed, beloved friends, Surrender is like the petals of the flower. They emerge in their own time. And one cannot necessarily see the causal connection of all that has gone before with the sweet nectar of perfect remembrance: the flowering of the soul that is no longer fearful and abides in the world awake, in peace, open—that through which the flow of Grace descends to touch the world. Surrender flowers from the only three things you can do: Desire, Intend, Allow. *Allow purification to occur.* Be willing to visit every dark corner of the mind. For, in Truth, it is not necessary to seek for Love, for Love already embraces you. But it *is* necessary to *seek for what is false*:

Where am I fooling myself?

Where am I committed to my image in the world?

Where am I committed to thinking for myself because underneath I don't truly trust that God loves me?

Where am I lying to myself or to others?

Where am I in denial?

Where do I need to understand what projection is?

Where do I need to understand more deeply how the viciousness of the ego works within my own mind?

Where am I pointing a finger outside of myself? Where am I denying my fear?

> *Where am I demanding that the world show up as I would have it, instead of surrendering to the structuring of the world in the Hands of the Holy Spirit that serves entirely my healing, my growth, my maturing into true responsibility?*

Indeed, beloved friends, in *The Way of Knowing* it is absolutely required that you pause often and look around you and say:

> *I abide in the perfection of a loving universe. Nothing can occur by accident. And where I am in this moment must be the perfect place for me to be. How can I find the doorway to stillness within, now?*
>
> *Where within me can I rest, in peace, and ask the Holy Spirit's guidance?*
>
> *Where, in this moment, am I clinging to another or to a thing?*
>
> *Where am I looking upon another person or another thing in this universe, claiming it is my possession?*

For what you do not give to be shared that you say you have loved, rest assured, beloved friend, in that moment, you are in the *viciousness of specialness*. The egoic mind believes that if it shares what it has, it loses. Therefore, in your world, when you perceive that someone or something has brought you a great source of comfort and love, and even security, to see that being shared elsewhere activates the fear of loss within the ego. Much like many of you might remember when you were teenagers, and you began "going" with a certain boy or certain girl in the seventh grade, and then two weeks later, they decided to "go" with someone else. Oh, how crushing it was, for the source of your love has been stripped from you! Never will you enjoy the smell of a flower again. Never will food taste good. There could surely be no one else in this universe that could provide you

Lesson Two

this great source of love and attention! Such is the immaturity of the child. Such the immaturity of many "children" who live in fifty- year-old bodies!

For, beloved friends, there is *no one* and *no created thing*—and the body-mind is just a created thing—that can be your *source* for Love. Relationship was never meant to be a device for finding sources for Love. Relationships were designed to be *holy*. And in holy relationship, two have come together—not to *get*, but to *create* out of loving devotion to the Grace that has awakened and purified their mind and hearts to the realization that only Love is Real, that there is no such thing as loss, and only Love is worthy to be celebrated. In Perfect Love, there is no possessiveness. In Perfect Love, there is perfect allowing. In Perfect Love—guess what? There isn't even you! There is only *God* loving *through you*!

Therefore, indeed, beloved friends, look around your very home. Is there an object that you could not see yourself giving up? If you truly want to hasten your awakening, go and give it away. For in the end, all that you *believe* you possess must be given away. And what you believe you possess is *the right to possessiveness,* the right to *be right*. When all things created as a substitute for the Reality of God have been rescinded or surrendered, then indeed, the flower has emerged and the sweet fragrance blesses everyone.

The Awakened Mind, then, the Mind that rests in Perfect Knowledge, looks upon all things that It has previously loved and sees that their *form* is not what is essential. It is the *essence* or the *content* that they express that matters. A beautiful painting, in and of itself, means nothing. Hit it with a hammer, light a match to it, throw dirt and mud on it, it's not the same. It is not the structure that matters. It is that in a timeless moment, you looked upon it, entered into relationship, and experienced the *essence of beauty* flowing through it. That essence or content is timeless. That essence or content is all around you! It sustains you! It breathes you! It is the Heart of your heart, the Soul of your soul, and the Mind of your mind!

Whenever you see any object, whether it be a body, a person, a mind, a thing, a flower, a pencil — it doesn't matter — when you feel what you call "being Love" evoked within you, it is because in that moment you've slipped between the cracks of the world, of the egoic mind, and you are experiencing the essential content of Reality: Love. You are experiencing *your own living true Reality*, for only Love is Real. When you come to see that that *Love* can be experienced at *any* moment, in *any* situation, with *anyone*, with *any* flower . . .

Well, I like roses but I don't like plumeria.

What nonsense! *Love* is what you should love! *Love* is what you should assume responsibility for detecting as it flows through each living thing. And a rock, in this sense, is a living thing. If it exists, within it is the good, the holy, and the beautiful. For only that which contains these things, which is the presence of God, can ever take form in the first place. *Nothing can be without the essence of what you are seeking!*

When you understand that it is the *content* that matters and not the *form*, suffering begins to finally be alleviated. You can begin to embrace the comings and goings of this transitory realm of the dream, as a dream. People enter your life and you embrace them and see the good, the holy, and the beautiful. They flow through their ever- changing changes, and then they die.

Now death can occur not just at the death of the body. Death occurs at any moment in relationship when another changes their mind. They may decide to leave you. They may decide to

Lesson Two

awaken, which means that the being that you were relating to is dead. A death has occurred, whether they leave you physically or not. That's really rather irrelevant. But when you come to attune yourself to the essential thread of Love that flows through all things, you are abiding in a deeper sense of Knowing. And whether an object, person, place, or thing enters your life and stays, or whether it flows through in a moment, or whether it flows through over the course of a lifetime, begins to be less and less relevant to you—less and less do you grasp at it.

Indeed, the Mind that is truly Awakened and rests in the eternality of Love that is all things, can lay the head of a loved one down, watch them take their last breath, feel a little wave of emotion pass through—all that is, is the disengagement of the auric fields at a physical level, that's all it is. So you let the little shudder of tears come through, you smile and go:

> *Oh, how sweet it was. How sweet it is, for Love is eternal. And wherever two minds have joined in Love, separation is absolutely impossible! So what's the big deal?*

And you allow something your world calls "death" to occur. And yet, *death is unreal* to the Mind that rests in the Perfect Peace of Knowing.

Beloved friends, you who have journeyed with me for longer than you would care to remember, it is always a journey of remembering and forgetting. That's what makes it your journey. You get a little glimpse or a taste of God, you tell the world that's what you want, but then, right away, you decide to forget it again so that you can experience the sweetness of *seeking*. You've become addicted to being a seeker. And to seek, you must first cleverly *push away* what is always yours anyway, in order to embark on yet another journey of seeking.

Finding — which is the same as resting in Knowledge, the same as Christ Consciousness, the same as Perfect Peace — *finding* requires giving up the game of seeking. Such a one cannot be known by the minds of the world. Such a one walks the world but inwardly is empty. Such a one is merely a conduit through which there are no longer any obstructions to the offering of God's Grace.

Indeed, beloved friends, you have journeyed with me for so long. Many of you have journeyed with me for so long that you've taught yourself the only way to be in relationship with me is to be *dependent* upon me. You have journeyed with me so long that you can't imagine, or won't let yourself imagine, being my equal. You won't let yourself imagine *letting go* of me. And yet, I say unto you, stepping into the fullness of Love requires *letting go of everything* you have possessed, even if that possession is me. For Love requires, finally, that you step through the door into the Kingdom and declare:

I am That One sent of the Father, created before all things. I am only Love. I am not my mind. I am not my body. I am not my personality. I'm not my history. I do not belong to the world. I am that vibration, that note of Love. I am the Christ, and as such do I abide. I love equally. I love without reservation. I love without possessiveness. I love only to extend the presence of God, that another might touch that place within themselves and be set free.

Love cannot possess. Wherever there is a trace of conditionality, rest assured, the viciousness of fear is in the ascendancy. Therefore, if you cannot surrender your pet, if you cannot surrender the object that sits upon your counter in your kitchen, if you cannot surrender a beloved into death, if you cannot surrender a beloved who changes their mind and decides to move to Antarctica, with celebration — rest assured, there is yet a place within you that requires correction. Correction requires

Lesson Two

willingness, *Intention*. And Intention requires your *Desire* that you dissolve even more deeply into the Love which *is* God.

Listen *very* carefully. Indeed, listen *very, very carefully* . . .

If you would know the Love of God, *you must BE that Love*. You can't know *about* it. You must literally *be* the presence of that Love. Only then do you know God.

This, then, is the essence of *The Way of Knowing*: *knowing by BEING that which you would have knowledge of—direct* experience, *direct* apprehension, by choosing to *be only that*. This is why Knowledge is a mystical experience. This is why True Knowing has an *immediacy*. It is not mediated through a theology, a religion, a philosophy, or any words. Words are just symbols of symbols. They are symbols of ideas, and ideas are a step still away from reality. One who knows Love knows it because every cell of their being is the *presence* of Love. *The Way of Knowing* culminates with your perfect resolve to BE the presence of the Love that God Is.

Now, if you would truly know Love, look upon the things that you fear. Discover them. Dig them up and out of yourself. Rest assured, any time you must look at another and analyze them, there is something you fear. Anything that pushes your buttons is a *sign* that something is still requiring your Love.

The Way of Knowing, beloved friends, can culminate *only* in the transformation of your mind to such a level of completion that you sit in your rocking chair and say:

> *There is only God. There has never been a separate me. There never could have been. There is only this moment in which Love can dance, can be celebrated, and can be extended. Father, what can we create this day that offers to the world the Grace of the*

good, the holy, and the beautiful?

I once described the highest state of consciousness, highest state of purification, as one in which the Son has awakened, and looks around him and sees to infinity. He sees not where He begins and the Father ends. For such is Their union, such Their marriage, such Their dance — the Unformed and the Formed, the Source and the Created, the Creator and the Creating — such this alchemical marriage that one cannot look and see where the soul ends and the Creator begins. And yet, the Awakened Mind knows that It is still the *Created* and It surrenders in perfect joy each moment,

Father, what would You have me do? What is Your Will for me?

Not in subservience, but because sanity has returned. It recognizes that It has never been the tiny gnat, whining and complaining and trying to make Life work the way it thinks it ought to work. It surrenders each moment. It dissolves in each moment. It abides in each moment. It knows that only the Love of God is Real,

Father, what would You have me do?

And It opens Itself and It receives the pebbles being dropped into Its pond, now not by Its own hand, but by the Hand of Grace, the perfect Hand of Mystery that I have called *Abba* — that Love, that creative Source, that Power, that Joy, that *sublime, sweet, sweet Mystery* that is constantly creating, for Love must extend Itself!

No longer is there concern or worry over the body. No longer is there concern or worry over the state of the world. No longer is there concern or worry over *anything*. There is only the eternal dance of Creation. The Awakened Mind *knows that It is a participant in Perfect Mystery,* and there are no longer any blocks or fears, whatsoever. And wherever you find yourself, if you're asked to be crucified, dead, and buried so you shock the world into realizing that there's something else besides "surviving," you do it! If it comes and it is given unto you to write books, you write them. So what? You're not attached. The flow of creativity is moving through you. If you're asked to take a simple picture that I placed in the mind of a certain artist and distribute it to fifteen million people, you simply do it, because you're no longer attached to your ego. If I ask you — if Love asks you through me or through another — to move to the far ends of the Earth to build a hut and to chant, you go and do it. What's the problem? There isn't any!

You are free as the wind. And only those born of the Spirit *know* the Spirit. The Spirit comes and goes where It does. You don't know where It came from. You don't know where It's going. You totally confuse the minds of mankind. *You are free!* For you listen to no other voice but the *Voice for Love!* What would you hold onto in a world of illusion?

Learn to discover the *content* that pervades all form, and you will taste the perfect freedom, the alleviation of pain that comes with attachment to the form — even your own. Even your very thoughts that yesterday you thought were true — today you've been taken even more deeply into Love, and what is in the past is allowed to pass away:

> *Yesterday I thought I knew God. Ha! Today I know God even more deeply because I've rescinded my need to be right about what I once thought I knew to be true. Father, give me even more of You! Father, give me even more of You! I want more! I desire more! You are infinite! You are my Beloved! I want only to die in You — ever more, ever deeper! Give me more of You — to taste You, to devour You, to die in You! More and more!*

And "more and more" becomes an eternal journey without end to a goal that has never changed — a journey with no distance, only the sublime experience of tasting God and then surrendering that taste in order to taste even more. Love comes to supplant fear. And learning to jump in order to receive the parachute becomes a delightful game to play.

When I decided to allow the crucifixion, I jumped.

> *Can I find my Father even more deeply here?*

For me, it was the culmination of a life in which I developed trust that my Father would always catch me. That journey, by the way, has never ended. And those of you that would come to where I am, rest assured, you best not waste a single moment. For I am continually dying more and more into God.

Therefore, indeed, beloved friends, we will end this short hour with this suggestion:

> *Where is* fear *still abiding in my mind? Is there anything that I still* fear? *Is it the death of a husband or a wife? Is it the growing up of a child? Is it the loss of a job? Is it being without shelter?*

Where is the edge of your fear?

> *Can I imagine abiding without a man in my life? Can I abide without a woman in my life?*

Hmm? This is nothing more than unhealed, what you call, mother and father issues. It is an *authority* problem. The Awakened abide only with God. They cannot any longer comprehend possessing or being possessed. They allow all things, trust all things. They love without reservation the one who stands before them as the embodiment of their very

Lesson Two

Beloved — *the content or essence which is the presence of God.* For when you look upon your brother or sister and see only Christ, you have seen with the Eyes of Christ. And Christ simply loves.

Therefore, indeed, beloved friends, be at peace.

Amen.

The Way of Knowing

Lesson Two Question and Answer Section

Following completion of the lesson, Jeshua often answers questions read to him on behalf of students.

Question: Jeshua, could you help us define *Knowledge* or *Knowing*?

Answer: Certainly. Knowing or Knowledge is an immediate quality of feeling. It transcends symbols. Knowledge is the result of revelation, and revelation is always intensely personal. That is, revelation flows across the gap that has seemed to exist between the Mind of God and the mind of the soul, or the Created. It cannot be mediated by symbols, since symbols are removed from Reality.

If you were to try to describe your revelation, you must immediately move into the realm of ideas and words. Words are symbols of symbols, and are thus twice removed from Reality. Ideas are what words are symbols of. Reality is unmediated. It is immediate. All of you have had many, many revelations. In an instant you simply see and know,

>   *Ah! I see. I know. Ah!*

Then you let it go. If someone were to ask you,

>   *Well, what just happened?*

then comes the *art* of trying to communicate through the mediation of words and ideas to give some sense of the revelation.

This is why even the greatest of your mystics, the greatest of

Lesson Two

your teachers, have tried to utter in words the essence of their revolution, or revelation of awakening (indeed, it is a revolution, too). Everything that I ever said, when I walked the earth as a man, anything that I have ever said to you, is the *artful attempt* to use symbols to point you in the direction of some *feeling* of the revelation that has occurred within my own mind of Christ. It's just the way it is; there's not much you can do about it. The attempt to communicate requires communion. And a teacher seeks the art-filled, art-guided way of evoking a state of communion between his and her mind and the mind of the student, in order to transfer the essence of revelation.

Knowing, then, has nothing to do with theology, religion, or a single text that has ever been given. Knowing, or Knowledge, is *immediate*. It is a Knowing by *being* that which the mind would seek to know.

When you touch Christ Mind, *you know it*. Because all of your beingness, the mind, the emotions, the physiology of the body — everything changes and comes into alignment. And in that moment, there is *no possibility* or even *memory* of fear. There is *nothing* but simply being present. It is timeless, it is eternal, it is peaceful.

Therefore, indeed, beloved friends, come to understand that *Knowing is what you seek*. And yet, Knowing does require that you begin by acknowledging that you are Christ. Remember always that this is the first and most fundamental act of purification. Your mind will tell you,

No, I'm a wretched sinner. No, I'm not there yet.

That is egoic thinking. You must notice it and say,

No. That cannot be the Truth of me. The Truth of me is that I am

the Holy Son of God — now.

You've dropped a pebble in the pond that creates ripples that will dissolve the patterns of fear that you once created to replace the Truth.

Knowing and Knowledge has nothing to do with belief. It is beyond belief — quite literally to the world mind. Knowing and Knowledge has nothing to do with theology or religion. It has everything to do with Reality.

That should be sufficient for now. We would suggest that you think deeply about what was said. It, in itself, will drop pebbles in the pond that help dissolve the resistance to Knowledge.

Question: Over the years we have seen many people who appear to get right to the crux of their blocks, and then they stop. After, they will pull away. And sometimes there can be projection, the forming of "glee clubs," and even outright attack. Could you speak to what's occurring there, as well as the best way to deal with it?

Answer: Well, indeed, beloved friend, I *never* experienced this when I was on the planet! Hmm.

Remember, always, that the world is the attempt of mind to create a *substitute* for the Kingdom of Heaven, to create a substitute for Reality. It is the *misuse* of power. It is a *waste* of the very gift that the Creator gives to the Created. It is *extremely* important to remember that as you walk the Earth, in the world (and there's a distinction between the world and the Earth: the *world* is what mankind has made in error), as you literally walk down your street, you are walking through a *field of illusion* in which *fear* seems to dominate. When everyone is fearful, everyone will believe that everyone is sane and normal. It is just

Lesson Two

taken to be the norm. And yet, the world is the opposite of the Kingdom.

Why is this important? Where fear has made a home in the mind, where any mind has become entranced with fear and doesn't even know it, it will cling to the foundational structure of belief upon which it is based:

> *I am guilty. I am separate from God. This is why I have to manipulate you, because I can't trust God. I won't find my security unless I figure out how to shape the world to give me what I think I need.*

Fear has many stepchildren. They are all vicious. And in the world you will encounter viciousness. You encounter it right now a thousand times *every day* — the store clerk who seems to be absent or not present with you as you put your groceries on the counter; the driver who honks at you because you are going three miles an hour slower than he or she wants you to. All of these are expressions of the insanity of fear. For where there is Love, there is a willingness to show up and be wholly present in the body-mind. Where Love is present, there is patience, trust, allowance, graciousness. The world you live in is permeated by fear — it's what made the world in the first place. Never deny this.

What then happens is this. *The first part of the mind which engages the spiritual journey is the ego.* It is the ego that first decides to listen to a tape of Jeshua ben Joseph. It is the ego that first opens to my presence. It is the ego that first picks up *A Course in Miracles*. Why? Because the ego is what is in charge. It has tried everything else. It's coming close to the time of its death and dissolution. And therefore, it looks upon spirituality as the one last-gasp attempt *to gain power and control.*

The ego always speaks first. So, you'll read a paragraph in *A Course In Miracles*, and immediately start thinking about it, immediately start pontificating about it. That's nothing but the ego! Those that would puff themselves up with many words *about* the *Course* are usually those least interested in *living* the *Course*. Do you see?

Therefore, what occurs is this. As any mind begins its "grand spiritual journey," what it's really being run by is the seeking for experiences that *it* has decided will *feel good*. Now, it will begin to have some experiences. It will go to workshops. It will read the *Course*. And guess what? The Holy Spirit seduces it. It does have moments of dissolution, little deaths, "Oh!" Spirit breaks through the ego. So the ego is attempting to use something for its own good, not even realizing that it's the very thing the Holy Spirit will eventually succeed at using in destroying the ego, the grip the ego has on the mind.

However, imagine that you are the defender of a castle. And around the castle you have five thousand acres. Now, out there in the fringes of your dominion, your kingdom, there are a few small hamlets. When the enemy comes to attack your castle, and you first hear that the enemy is amassing at your borders, there's a little fear:

> *Well, okay. So we'll give it a few hamlets. Big deal. We'll let Genghis Khan have the hamlet at the furthest edge.*

But the closer Genghis Khan comes to the castle, the more ferocious Genghis Khan seems to be, the more the ramparts are pulled up, the more the soldiers come to line the fortress, the more you prepare yourself with your cannons, machine guns, and what have you. You'll do anything to defend the heart of the castle.

Lesson Two

Now, in Truth, there was never a Genghis Khan. There were merely angels on white horses coming to bring the petals of Love and healing, coming to teach you that you need not build fortresses at all, that you can let the castle go and live in the meadows in the Father's Kingdom. However, those angels are turned into ferocious monsters that look like Genghis Khan and,

Surely, they're out to destroy me.

Never underestimate the viciousness of the ego. This will happen time, and time, and time, again. As, on the one hand, the egoic mind that says it's on a spiritual path will engage its practices and—oh my!—it will just talk and talk and talk and talk, and read and study, and travel, and do workshops. It will do all of these things, never realizing that it is really about trying to defend its inner castle—the place where the ego is still in authority.

And as Love begins to penetrate and take over the hamlets, it gets closer and closer. And sometimes, the heat is too much. The power of the ego is still too strong and it pushes Love away. Now, how do you push Love away? By *calling it* something else. By seeing it as Genghis Khan:

How dare you ask me to question my own views on sexuality! Why, I know the truth! This is the way it must be!

And then, that very mind will go to a workshop and hear about denial, projection, attack. It will hear all these nice theories and it will go,

Yes, yes. Ha, ha, ha, ha! Oh, yes. Well, hmm, hmm, hmm.

But boy! When its own inner castle is threatened, and reactivity rears its head, and it sends its soldiers to the wall to keep Genghis Khan out ...

It takes much, much experience in the pathway of purification to come to recognize that *where there is reaction, there is fear. What is not Love is fear,* and nothing else. At any time, when you have enmity with a brother or sister, that is, you're getting your buttons pushed, you've got a problem or an issue . . . when you do not go to them directly, but rather seek out others to talk to, you will seek an accomplice—what you have called a "glee club":

> *Let's get together and sing the chorus of what's wrong with that person over there. This way, we both get to be right.*

At any time that you think you have an issue with someone, and you do not go to them directly to discuss it with openness, to discuss it with the goal being growth and learning, you may rest assured that you have rushed into your castle and sent your soldiers to the wall. And you are *delaying* your healing and awakening. Any time you seek an accomplice, you have lost and the ego has won. Because why? Because fear has won!

> *Oh, gee. I've really had this issue. Gosh, what you did is really pushing my buttons. But I'm not going to talk to you about it. I'll go find somebody else who's also had their buttons pushed. We'll get together and discuss what's wrong with you, so we get to be safe.*

Where? Inside the castle of illusion.

So, as Love penetrates the veils, the hamlets, of the kingdom of the ego, it gets closer to the castle. The ego seeks to fortify its boundaries. Why? Because the ego *is* fear itself.

Lesson Two

It takes *much* experience — *much* maturity — at *truly owning* that what's occurring under your skin is *yours*. Are you committed to Love and healing and growth? Or are you committed to keeping the status quo in place? Fear grips you [snaps fingers] that fast! It causes all manner of reactivity, projection, attack. That's just the viciousness of the insane ego.

Now this has occurred, as you know, in the nature of your journey with me, for the two of you specifically over the last nine years, many times. Why? Because your work, both within yourselves, and therefore within the outer work, the service that you give to others, is *about* dissolving the castle. That is what the essence of Shanti Christo is: *dissolving the deepest, innermost bastion of strength in which the ego is running the show.*

This work that I engage with you in is *the deepest work possible*. It is *only* about the Atonement. The Atonement is not to make you feel good. It is literally to purify the mind of the grip of the ego, so that God can possess, if you will, your mind, your life, your being — so that you can return to being a creator of the good, the holy, and the beautiful.

This means, first of all, that this work attracts those who are at various stages of their desire to awaken. Many of them are at the egoic stage. What is the egoic stage of spirituality? It is that stage in which the ego knows it's tried everything else. It's tried to make money. It's had relationships. It's done its drugs in your culture. It's had too many hours of TV. It's tried *everything* to stay in power, and it perceives that perhaps in the "spiritual life" it will finally gain the power it seeks over what it perceives to be Genghis Khan on the borders of its dominion.

Therefore, many will first be attracted to my message, through this, my beloved brother — through the various forms of the work that I have guided you to learn, to become skillful in. But the first level of attraction is always *the seeking of a new power*. The rattles will come when the hamlets begin to be attacked. And depending on the strength that the ego has—no matter how much so-called spiritual journeying one has done—the strength of the ego within the castle will be perceived by those who pull away, by those who need to project and attack, those that need to form glee clubs—these are *signs*. They can merely teach you to learn more deeply the subtle nuances of how egoic consciousness works. This, in turn, improves your ability to teach.

This is why whenever you feel attacked, what matters first of all is to recognize the mechanics that are at play.

> *Oh! If someone's attacking me, they must be in fear, since there is only Love or fear. If there is an issue that I know they have, and they're not coming to talk to me about it, this only shows how deeply fear is actually running their life.*

Now, the first thing, then, is *compassion* and *prayer*. Hmm? Seeing them as healed, seeing them as whole, asking for guidance,

> *Should I go speak to them?*

Yes. No. The Holy Spirit will let you know.

The second thing is, if I'm *feeling* attacked, let me drop *them*, bring attention back to myself,

What's feeling attacked in me?

For only egoic consciousness can *be* attacked. Christ cannot be attacked—it's impossible. Christ just laughs. Christ may choose to take the body-mind away from those who are

Lesson Two

dangerous to the body-mind, but *Christ* never feels attacked. So it's a great offering, and in this sense they've become your savior — not because they're enlightened, but because you can use the situation to more deeply see what *you* may yet be afraid of.

Now, what's the crux of all this? Anyone who truly wants God will seek out situations of teaching and learning that literally create a context for the greatest fire, the greatest purification, the greatest heat. Why? Because they want to get the gold melted down so it can be reshaped by the Hand of God.

If you are not experiencing other minds saying that you're wrong, if you're not experiencing other minds being activated by the life you're living, you better take another look. What's really running you? Are you afraid to speak and live your truth? Are you afraid to choose Love over fear? Are you afraid to look different to other minds? True meekness stands out like a sore thumb, for the meek know that they do not know. The meek trust the Holy Spirit. The *ego* is out to get others to like it. The *soul* wants only God.

Therefore, remember that when you are being attacked, you have, in the palm of your hand, a great gem that is totally priceless. For you can deepen your own embodiment of Christ Consciousness. You can learn more deeply the subtle nuances of how egoic consciousness dominates the mind, whether yours or another's. You can learn and learn and learn, and thereby become a greater teacher, capable of serving the Atonement.

Now, to come back to our analogy of Genghis Khan attacking the kingdom, think of all things as a vibration of energy. When two people come together in relationship, or when ten thousand come together, they come together because there's a certain level of accord or resonance. Now Genghis Khan can come so far into the kingdom and everybody in the kingdom and in the castle is relatively okay:

> Yes, yes. Well, the war is out there on the farthest reaches of our kingdom. We can still party. Isn't this great? Oh, yes. Ha, ha, ha!

Genghis Khan comes closer. And now, every mind must make a choice:

> What am I committed to?

If, for example, there is conflict in a relationship, if one mind in the relationship refuses to go to the other and say:

> Gosh, I'm really having this issue. We need to go into this because I recognize that if I have an issue, there's something here that I need to learn.

If they're not willing to do that, they've reached their edge, what you have called the "crux of their obstacle." They've looked within, the situation has flushed something up, but *now*, they make a choice — without even knowing that they've made it. Their choice is to defend their castle. They will then spin out and leave you. They'll spin out and form glee clubs, they'll project, they'll attack, whatever it is. It's all harmless insanity. It only means that they've missed an opportunity and will have to come back around at another time, through more painful experiences, to look at the very issue that they aren't willing to go through. They've come to their edge of their ring of fear. And fear has won the day.

That's their loss. But it need not be yours. For anyone, at anytime, is *free* to learn more deeply about forgiveness and Love, about patience, about allowing, about transcending, about growing in the maturity of embodying Christ. The mind

Lesson Two

that reaches a certain stage of maturity is really no longer concerned with projection and attack — in fact, begins to relish it. For that mind knows that greater power must be coming through it if it is activating other minds. Do you see? The ego seeks safety. The Christ Mind serves the Atonement — and has fun doing it.

Now this means that in the stages of Shanti Christo, as we began this work some nine years ago, going on ten years ago, from the day that I first came to this, my beloved brother, the goal has always been to fulfill my agreement with him to bring him fully into God Consciousness, to journey with him until my obligation as his teacher had ended. Now, within that, the secondary effect is to create a work that allows a context in which others *also* can join with me, can enjoin the process of awakening. That's what Shanti Christo is, the creation of a context that can invite the entire humanity, the entire family of humanity, into the process of dissolving the innermost castle where the ego has built its fortress. That is what it must serve at all times. This means that the more powerfully you are doing that, rest assured, it means the more you will probably find people coming and going, find yourself being projected on. It's always been that way in the world, where any Ray of Light gets too strong and too clear. Do you see?

So in the future, those of you — and there will be more and more playing with you at deeper and deeper, more mature levels of commitment... when you find yourself attacked by others in the world, *remember this must mean you're on the right track*! It doesn't mean you're going to be destroyed. No one will destroy this work. It doesn't mean you're going to be hurt. You can't be hurt. You're going to succeed. It simply means that that's the way it is when Light penetrates darkness. Each mind *must be given freedom* to protect its castle, to wait for another day, or to choose to step into deeper maturity, deeper commitment to the great dissolution and death of egoic control that growth in Christ Mind requires.

So when people come and go, give it no thought. Merely love and keep growing yourselves in Christ. The only reason you've achieved the level of miracle-mindedness and success that has been achieved is because you have matured enough to recognize that this journey must first be *your own*.

Let each one who comes to join with you remember that the growing success of Shanti Christo requires *their commitment* to penetrate their own castles, whether they be your employees, whether they be your Board of Directors, whether they be your members. Those who say they want to see the success of this venture *must* be fully committed to the ongoing process of *birthing Christ in themselves*.

Does that sufficiently answer your question?

Yes.

Lesson Two

PERSONAL NOTES

The Way of Knowing

PERSONAL NOTES

Lesson Three

Lesson Three

Now, we begin.

And indeed, again, greetings unto you, beloved and holy friends. We come forth to abide with you — we come forth to abide with you through this, our beloved brother — in order to enjoin you, yet again, in this year of *The Way of Knowing*.

Remember always that Knowledge is perfectly certain. Knowledge is that which is unchanging, unchangeable, and unchanged forever. Knowledge *is* Reality, and Reality is Love. Knowledge is the essence of your being — Knowledge, the essence of your soul.

If anyone says unto you,

I do not know,

they are a liar and a hypocrite, though I would not suggest that you use those terms in your communication with them. But rather, whether in your own life or in relationship with a friend, wherever *doubt* seems to arise in the mind, remember only this: this mind is not currently choosing Reality. It must, therefore, be choosing something else. And the something else can only be that experience, that world, of the ego. For we use the term "ego" to differentiate that state of awareness that is characterized by *confusion* wearing the *mask of certainty*. When anyone says unto you,

I don't know,

whenever the thought arises in your own mind,

I don't know,

rest assured, that in that moment, that mind — your mind — is choosing to be *other* than what it is.

And what is it, then, that you know?

> *I and my Father are One. I am intimately connected with that very Source from which has sprung forth all things.*

Because this is the Truth, because it is the Truth of your being, this means that for any situation that requires a decision, you have within yourself access to Perfect Knowledge. And Perfect Knowledge seeks to extend Itself. And extension requires the realm of manifestation, the realm of form, the realm of individuation. Therefore, *you* — as a body and as a mind, abiding in space and time on a tiny planet — *you are* Reality's decision to manifest Itself in form, for no other reason than to extend Its own nature. The happiness of the soul depends on its decision to extend only that which *is* Loving.

Because *you* are the manifestation of Reality Itself, of Knowledge Itself, of Love Itself, it must mean that in any given moment, there is within you a part of the mind that yet remains free from the ego's authority — that part in which there already abides *perfect peace;* that part of the mind in which there already abides *perfect certainty;* that part of the mind in which there already abides *the willingness to extend Love without attachment.* There is already within you that part of the mind that can deliver up to you the answer for each decision, the answer that helps to *extend Love,* first into your own beingness, and then through it. For you can only *give* what you first *receive.* And in your giving, your receiving is completed.

Therefore, indeed, beloved friends, if you would look to see what the purpose of your life is, it is quite simple. Being only Love, you can have no other purpose than to extend the treasure of your very Self. Christ is God's only creation. Christ

Lesson Three

is that medium, if you will, through which the unfathomable, mysterious, beyond-comprehension Source that I have called *Abba* (and goes by many names), extends Itself into the creation of temporary forms to reflect, throughout the Universe, that which the Universe Itself is made of — where it comes from, what it is enveloped within, and that to which it eternally returns.

Because *you*, like a wave unto the ocean, have been birthed from that Reality, emerging from that Reality, you are one with it. Therefore, you *are* Christ Eternal. That is unchanging and unchangeable forever. Within you, then, even in this very moment, there abides a part of the mind that already knows the Truth that sets all things free. That part of the mind can be accessed at *any* time by *any* one under *any* condition. It does not require years of cultivation, although in the field of time it can appear that you're getting better and better at it, simply because you're *enjoying* it more and more and giving value to the fear-based egoic ways of arriving at decisions less and less.

That part of the mind is like an empty and open channel. Nothing can obscure its purity — *nothing*. Nothing you have ever done, nothing you have ever thought, nothing you've ever miscreated obscures the perfect silence, the utter purity, of your connection with the Source of your being. For Love is always connected to Itself.

What does this mean, then? First, anyone who truly enjoins *The Way of Knowing* must make a decision to accept the Atonement for themselves:

> *I am One with my Creator — now. I choose to fulfill my purpose by extending only the reflection of my Self, and I am but Love.*

Secondly, anyone who would enjoin *The Way of Knowing* must

also look and embrace the very fact that their attention is involved in the world of space and time, the world of the body itself. But in *The Way of Knowing*, the world of space and time is *seen* differently. Rather than as something that exists *external* to the mind itself—something which has a power over the mind itself, something that is therefore to be feared, something that one must be conformed to—the things of space and time are seen and embraced as that which is given of the Creator to the Son, to the Daughter, in order to be utilized as devices for assisting Christ to extend Love . . . whether it be a pencil or a computer or a trip to your grocery store or a party in which you invite your friends to come and play. All things finally come to be seen as having only one purpose: *the extension of Love.*

Imagine a business person sitting down to negotiate the closing of a deal, who goes to that part of the mind that is sane and says,

> *What price should I place upon this land that I am about to sell to this other corporation?*

And while his accountants and realtors have been telling him that the property is worth one million dollars, he goes within. And the answer comes,

> *Ask only $250,000 and ask that another $300,000 be donated to such-and-such a charity.*

In *your* world, which is the world of insanity, the business man would say,

> *Oh no, I can't do that. I cannot listen to that voice.*

But in *The Way of Knowing*, in the way of enlightenment, the businessman smiles and says exactly what was received. When

Lesson Three

the shock on the other person's face settles down, they will be quite happy to know that they've saved a lot of money, for in *their* world, they think that the only way to *have* is to *possess*. But in *The Way of Knowing*, and in the way of Reality, the only way to *have* is to *give*.

Now, you are like that businessman. You abide in the world in which *the business of your Reality is to extend only Love*. Be you, therefore, not afraid of the world. For the world of space and time, when seen through the eyes of the enlightened soul that accepts its oneness with God, the world of space and time is perfectly benign and has *no purpose whatsoever except to serve Christ in the extension of Love*. And this is why anyone who comes to answer only the Voice for Love miraculously finds that the Universe comes to support that one in ways that the egoic mind can never understand. Miracles do occur as Creation flows from a mind unencumbered with the pressures of trying to make life go the way it thinks it needs it to go.

And here we begin to touch upon the essence of my teaching,

I need do nothing.

This is not a passive state, by the way, of just accepting the fact that:

I need to do nothing, and I'll just show up, and follow my impulses and not think too deeply or wonder what I'm doing. I really don't need to do anything, since none of it matters.

That's not it at all. It means quite *actively* to learn and master the art you do *need* to do nothing; to find that spaciousness within you in which you are willing to allow that channel within you that is eternally connected to your Source to be the vehicle through which you receive your guidance, in the pure

59

recognition that you have no purpose—save the extension of Love.

It is not your purpose to survive as a body-mind. It is not your purpose to keep the same house you've had for the last twenty years. It is not your purpose to be in relationship with this person or that person for the entirety of the life of the body-mind. It is not your purpose to accomplish great things. It is not your purpose to be wealthy. It is not your purpose to do *anything* except be that conduit through which Love extends Itself.

As you come, truly, to allow Love to be your greatest Beloved, as you set aside all other idols—the need to hold onto the house, the need to have certain dollars in the bank, the need to have certain people in your life—as you come to see that all of that is part of the world of illusion, as you come to love *Love*, you will have come to love *yourself*. For you *are* Love, and only this. And as you come to love Love as your Beloved, more and more, you will discover that you are guided on a path of miracles in which more power, if you will, seems to be getting extended through you. You'll begin to witness that the Universe seems to support you, more and more, in ways that you could have never imagined.

Out of that you might, indeed, see the life of the body-mind changing—the car you drive, the home you live in, the quality of the beings that come into your life. And yet, you will be unattached to these things, for you will not see them as ends in themselves, but merely as the proof that the great Wisdom of Love that underlies all things is connecting you to new forms, new contexts, because It knows that now It can flow *through* you more powerfully, more certainly, more maturely, more wisely.

Lesson Three

Therefore, seek not to improve your life by adding even one cubit unto your stature, but rather, seek to improve your life by *realizing your nature as Love*. How do you do that? By recognizing that in each moment you are in the right place at the right time.

And *this* is the moment in which Love can be remembered, can be restored, and can be extended. *This* is the moment in which you can decide to listen only to the voice within you that *knows* how to extend Love.

Beloved friends, in *The Way of Knowing*, the illusion that there is something to seek vanishes. In *The Way of Knowing*, the mind is liberated from the misperception that there's something wrong going on in the world. The mind is so liberated that it knows as long as it chooses Love, as long as it follows the mysterious, quiet voice within its own heart, that the choices it makes, the decisions it embraces, the actions it takes, the thoughts that it thinks, cannot help but serve in the further awakening of every one and every thing, so *perfect* is the Love that embraces the whole of Creation—God!

You have heard me say to you, therefore, many times, that wherever you know a fearful thought, it can only mean that you are not thinking "rightly," that is, you are not thinking with the Mind of God. And God is but Love. If a million dollars were to come to you one of your days, as Christ, you would say:

This must be the perfect experience for me now. How can I extend Love in this moment?

And if, in the next day, your wallet is perfectly empty, the enlightened Mind of Christ says:

This must be the perfect event for me to be experiencing now.

The Way of Knowing

How can I extend Love in this moment?

The changing can never be the source of peace. The world of form — whether dollars in a bank, houses, cars, people, friends, lovers, pets, plants, and all of the rest — the world of form, in itself, can never be the source of perfect freedom. These things arise and pass away and are like ephemeral shadows, wisps of foam dancing in an ocean. When the mind becomes identified with the *form*, that mind *suffers*. When the mind is liberated from attachment to form, it is free, for it is identified only with *content*, or simply the Reality of Love.

In any given moment, you have the power within you to experience the Reality of Love, unobstructed, unmediated — *now* — without need of magical means, without need for the Universe to arrange itself in any certain way, whatsoever. In any given condition, you have within yourself the power to decide to, literally, *feel* and *experience Love*. Love, then, or the experience of it, is a decision. It is not something earned, and it is not something created. It is that which is eternally present *now* as the very identity of your being, the very Life of your being, the existence of your being.

Once, I said to this, my beloved brother:

> *Merely stand, with arms outstretched and palms up. Open the heart deeply, and ask whatsoever you will. And it shall be given you. But ask as the Awakened Christ, asking from that place that knows only Love is Real.*

Therefore, take just a moment, *right now!* Stand from wherever you are, and take your arms outstretched with palms turned Heavenward. Think about your own heart for just a moment, and simply ask to *feel* and *know* the Reality of Love's presence. Breathe it into your heart. Open the cells of the body. Open the

Lesson Three

mind and simply *receive* what is available.

Good! And now you can allow yourself to sit down again, if you wish, or continue to stand. If you think you "didn't get it," you're simply fooling yourself. It requires only this. And perhaps we should then give you this as a meditation to do in *The Way of Knowing*. Arise from your chairs, and at least once a day, stand with your arms outstretched and the palms up and say simply:

I open and receive the Reality of Love for my Self — now!

You see, *Self-love* is the pathway to perfect peace. Self-love opens all the doors. Self-love dissolves every illusion. I'm not speaking of love for the illusions of the egoic mind with which you have become identified. I am not saying that you should say:

I love my self because I now have x amount of dollars in the bank. I love my self because I have a wonderful husband or wife. I love my self because I have a great dog.

No.

I love my Self.

The Self that is beyond time is that Self from which even the body has emerged.

Whenever you are in doubt, whenever your energy seems to have dropped, try a dose of *celebrating*. A simple dose of celebrating that you are in a perfect Universe, you abide as Love, and the very fact that you have a body that has emerged out of consciousness in order to be used to extend only Love is pretty miraculous. And you are free to celebrate that simple, essential Truth in any moment. Then ask:

> *Great! Who can I extend Love to now? How can I experience Love now?*

It's all much simpler than you think.

In *The Way of Knowing*, there is Knowing. If that statement seems puzzling to you, contemplate it as a meditation:

> *In 'The Way of Knowing', there is Knowing.*

There is no more powerful state of consciousness to act from than the state of Knowing. For indeed, beloved friends, if you truly accepted yourself as Christ, you would *know* that you cannot fail. And if you cannot fail, what would you do with your time? If you knew you could not possibly fail, that the Universe will support you completely at all times, as you choose *only* to act, to do, to think in a way that extends Love, would you be living where you're currently living? Would you be doing with your time what you're currently doing? . . . many of you because you think you must survive *first*, in order to find a way to teach only Love.

In *The Way of Knowing*, the Christ Mind recognizes it has no purpose, whatsoever, except to extend Love. The body-mind need not survive more than the next moment, if in that next moment you have extended Love and your guidance is,

> *Time to be beamed up.*

Those that know that only Love is Real are not concerned with what they eat and what they drink. For these things come into the body and leave through the body. They are concerned only with whether or not that which they consume for the sake of

Lesson Three

the body was consumed in Love. For *Love* is what allows the transmutation of anything that comes into the physical system and allows it to be turned to that which supports the energetic wholeness of the physical system itself.

It is far greater, by the way, to have what you call a bottle of Scotch for breakfast in a state of total Christed Love, than it is to have nine thousand vitamins spread before you with one tiny little fearful thought. So, that's just an aside and something for you to think about.

For you see, it is fear that causes you to be unable to digest what you place in the body — the body of the emotions, or the body of the mind. It is what causes stress in the subtle system of the body: the emotional body, the mental body, the causal body — the subtle nonphysical bodies. What causes the greatest problem is your refusal to *digest* what you've taken in. And just as food is a physical substance taken into the body, an *experience* of any kind is a "food" that has been called to the soul. Anything that arises that cannot pass through you, through your willingness to embrace it with Love, to feel it completely, will cause "indigestion" of the physical, emotional, mental, and causal beings or bodies.

Therefore, indeed, beloved friends, learn to digest *all things* in Love. Learn to digest the traffic jam in Love. Learn to digest the dying of a pet in Love. Learn to digest an apple in Love. Learn to digest a hurtful thought in Love. Learn to digest a misperception that there's something wrong with the world around you with Love. Transform all things by the power of your only Reality.

And now, we would shift ever so slightly and ask you to join with us. For I want to ask of you: What is it that you have refused to digest in *this one incarnation?* Was it an unfairness bestowed upon you by your mother or father? Was it the "bad break" at the office in which you got passed up for a promotion? What is it in your life that remains undigested?

There! Something has come into the mind. Trust it. Stay with that one thought, that one picture, that one memory. For it has arisen in the conscious mind to be healed and transformed *now*. Bring your attention to it in this very moment. Look upon it, breathe with the body, and say simply within the mind:

> *I choose now to fully digest this by bringing Love to it, by actually loving the event just as it was — loving the picture, the memory, the thought, just as it is.*

If you wish, you can stand with your arms out wide and your palms turned Heavenward and receive the Love that transmutes all things. *Breathe* that Love! *Feel* that Love in and through that picture, that memory, that feeling — whatever it is that's occurring for you, until it literally dissolves. And if you don't feel that happening, even in your body, there's a part of you that's *resisting* letting go of what has been undigested. And if that is the case, you need to ask yourself:

> *Why do I need to uphold my illusory perception about this event? What in me is committed to withholding my Love?*

If you wish, we would highly suggest that you spend some time each day asking the same question:

> *What is it that I've not been willing to digest about this life and about this world? Where am I refusing to bring my Love?*

Is it to your government? Is it to your Internal Revenue Service? Hmm? Is it to the mate? Is it to the children? To the pet? To the school system? What is it that you have refused to bring your

Lesson Three

Love to?

For you see, the greatest joy in life is to be the Lover of Life. For as you love, you experience Love. Therefore, do unto others what you would have done unto yourself.

And is that not to be loved? And when you choose to love in any given moment, you are the one who gets to receive the benefits of Love first. It is an immediate experience, and it cannot be taken from you. You are free to "juice yourself" any time you want by choosing only to Love. In any given condition, you are the presence of that one to whom all power under Heaven and earth has been given, not just to extend Love as a duty, for it is not a duty, it is a *pleasure*. It is the *supreme pleasure* that can be experienced in the depth of any mind, whether you happen to be in the world of space and time or, like me, out of it.

You are the one that can experience Love and let your cup overflow. You are the one who can *enjoy* each and every moment, regardless of the conditions. For the conditions are only the interpretations of the egoic mind. All events are neutral. They are there for you to *love*, that you might *experience Love*! That's really how simple it is. It has always been that way, and it will never change. You are the Lover. The world can be the reflection of your Beloved.

Let each moment, then, find you in the simple, quiet, inner enjoyment that comes from the decision *to love*. To love the taking out of the garbage. To love the rain that hits the windows. To love the crying of the child. To love, to love, to love! Love embraces all things, allows all things, trusts all things, and therefore transcends all things. And that is the power that abides within you when you finally choose to be That One who Knows.

Look well, then, this day and seize this day. Beloved friends, *where* can you simply change your mind and bring Love to something that you've been withdrawing Love from?

Well, I've got to go to the office.

No, you don't! You are *choosing* to go to the office. You might as well *love* it!

Where, O beloved friends, are you being presented with opportunities to experience Love coursing through every cell of your being this day? What can prevent you from experiencing Love if it is not but your own decision? For in *The Way of Knowing*, the liberated Mind of Christ knows,

There is nothing outside me.

And with that, peace be unto you always, O Holy Child of God.

Amen.

Lesson Three

Lesson Three Question and Answer Section

Question: How do I not keep one love for myself and yet continue loving myself?

Answer: Indeed, beloved friend, it is a question well asked about a very subtle, but important, point as one comes to live a fully Christed Life. When I said not to keep one love for yourself, I was indicating that the egoic mind looks upon forms of any kind, whether it be person, place, or thing, and projects its love onto it, and then misperceives it as a source of Love.

There is nothing outside of you that serves as a source for Love. One of the great tricks of the mind, in the human experience, is that when the mind experiences Love, it forgets that it is experiencing It because it is making a decision to do so. It believes, then, that something outside of itself has had the power to change its own state. But this is not so. Therefore, those "loves" become attachments. They are idols. And that would be another word to use for the love that you should not keep for yourself.

Make not an idol of that through which you've experienced Love. Make not an idol of the great physical lover who gives you ten thousand orgasms in a single night—hmm? Do not keep that love for yourself. Do not seek to possess that one for your own selfish reasons. Do not seek to possess the money that comes to you and to hoard it up in barns to save against a rainy day. For that will only ensure that you will experience a rainy day.

Keep not one love for yourself. How, then, can you experience self-love if you're not keeping one love for yourself? Beloved friend, the answer is just the opposite. How can you experience self-love when you are caught up in trying to possess the loves that you would see as outside of yourself? Self-love requires surrendering attachment to the illusions that you have formed about those things — persons, places, or things — that you think are sources of Love. Think about it. It's a hundred-and-eighty-degree turn.

You do not love yourself, you see, by bringing more of the things into your life that you say you love. That is a great mistake. If you say,

> Oh, I absolutely love shoes.

You will then see that "shoeness" is a source that has a magical power that can trigger a change of heart and mind in you. And you will then take the dollars that flow to you, and every time your energy drops, you'll think,

> Oh, shoes!

And you'll run out and you'll buy yet another pair to get a temporary fix. You will think you have loved yourself by giving the *things* to yourself that you think you love. That is not truly self-love, although it is a great beginning point when working with someone who is totally insane; that is, totally caught up in egoic consciousness — so much so that they won't even allow themselves to enjoy their egoic state of consciousness. It is very wise, then, to say to one,

> Oh, you like ice cream? Very well, give yourself total permission to have all the ice cream you want.

It's not the ice cream that matters. It's the act of recognizing and re-cultivating the ability to *feel* and *receive enjoyment* — that's all.

Lesson Three

But as that begins to mature, you begin to see through the transparency of the things of the world. You come to see that you can give yourself enjoyment by taking a deep breath, stretching the arms out with the palms up, and receiving Love. Nothing has to change around you. You don't have to eat anything. You don't have to sex the body. You don't have to accomplish anything great in the world. You need only receive the presence of Love.

Self-love, then, actually comes to grow the more you release attachment to the idols of love that you have created in the world. A woman who "loves" her garden in the back yard because *it* gives *her* so much enjoyment—not quite true. She *decides* to bring enjoyment to the act of gardening, while the neighbor next door can merely have a garden to try to keep up with the Jones's, but hates every moment of it.

It is not the garden that creates joy. It is the decision to *bring* joy to the activity of gardening. And then, you see, the lady can never leave her house, can never move away, because,

> *Oh, my god! I can't give up my garden. It's the source of my greatest joy!*

And that woman stays in the same house until the day she dies, pushing away her dreams of seeing Europe. Pushing away her dreams of swimming with a dolphin. Why? Because the garden has become the thing with the power to give her joy.

> *Hold not one love for yourself.*

Let it go. Let it become transparent. Do not be attached to it. Learn to recognize that in any given moment, when you are experiencing Love, it's because you've *decided* to. *You* are the one who has brought enjoyment to the context of the moment.

The Way of Knowing

The thing, in itself, is neutral. Power is not outside of you.

How, then, can you let go of the loves of the world that you have created and still love yourself? By holding what I've just shared with you, by sitting with it, by putting it into practice, by recognizing, more and more deeply, that when you are doing what you love, it's because you have first decided to open your heart in Love, and then take action. If you love to sing, it is the Love that is present first. And then you sing. The singing doesn't cause love for yourself.

Therefore, indeed, beloved friend, contemplate well what I have shared with you. For the great paradox of the mystical Christed Mind is to see that there's nothing to hold onto in the world because there is no world. There is only the Reality of Love extending Itself through the temporary context of form. If you find yourself loving to make music, know that it is *from Love* that you are *choosing* to be a music maker, temporarily.

That should be sufficient for now.

Question: Since we do not know what our brother or sister needs, is it possible that the Holy Spirit would guide us to say and do things that others would react vehemently to, such as You did when You yelled and got angry at the moneychangers? Is it true that we can't put a lid on how the guidance of the Holy Spirit would sound or look?

Answer: By its very nature, the guidance of the Holy Spirit comes from beyond the realm of ideas and perceptions that the mind identifies itself with. If you think of a room in a house as being where you normally abide, you know all the furniture, you've identified it all, you've defined it, it's under your control. In such a room, when you go to access the answer for a problem or a situation that has arisen, you can only go to what

Lesson Three

you already know.

That is what the egoic mind tries to do, even when it begins to receive into its "room" new ideas — spiritual ideas, metaphysical ideas, religious ideas, magical means ideas. It still is in the realm of the known and so, when a situation comes up, it rummages around the room looking for something it knows is already there. And it looks for what it thinks will be the device, the word, the phrase, the action, that is the right thing. But this is the very same thing as saying that you already know what you need to say or do. But you do not have that knowledge in the room in which the ego lives.

That space or channel, that we spoke of earlier, through which Love can inform your decisions, requires that you recognize it is *beyond* the context of the room that you're used to living in. The mind, as you know it — your daily mind — can operate *only* in a closed universe of what it already knows.

Therefore, in a given situation, the Holy Spirit may have said to you,

> *Take this homeless brother into your house and fix him a good meal.*

And so, you've done it. Now, ten years later, there is another homeless man outside your door. You rummage around in the *past*, and you see that once you brought this person in and you fed him,

> *Oh, this must be the solution because this is my "homeless person" tape. I just pulled it out of my dresser drawer in my egoic mind.*

You've forgotten that there was a time when a homeless man

appeared and you didn't know what to do. You let go of everything you thought you knew and you asked in prayer. This same way of *not knowing* is the ultimate state of *Knowing*. Knowing that the egoic mind does *not* know is the source of *powerful Knowing*.

Therefore, could it be the case that the Holy Spirit would guide you to say or do something that might cause others to act, or react, vehemently? Indeed, beloved friends—yes! But remember this: the Holy Spirit's guidance is not what is causing another to react vehemently. Their *own mind* causes that, because they are not committed to healing and to Love. Any reaction that is not the extension of Love must be fear, and nothing else. Any form of attack or judgment can come only from fear, and not from Love.

Therefore, when I felt guided to approach the moneychangers in front of my Father's holy temple, I was not guided to say:

> *Excuse me, could we have a slight conference here? I would like to express a slight opinion, and of course, you're totally free to do what you will, because you're actually very powerful, rich beings and I am just a lonely Essene. But if you'd just give me a minute, I'd just like to share my thought.*

No. I was guided to move with great power, to literally act in the ways that some would call violence—not that I hurt anybody, but I overturned their tables and I yelled deeply that,

> *You have made my Father's house a den of thieves!*

Now, that got their attention. Why? Because the Holy Spirit saw that those minds engaged in those activities could respond only to a powerful energy, since they idolized power, itself. They were always putting themselves in the position of having more

Lesson Three

power than the people who came to the temple. So, what was required was someone who put themselves in a greater source of power and demonstrated that the moneychangers were not as powerful as they thought. They couldn't imagine, before that moment, that anybody would upset their apple cart. But through that act, it began to create what you might call a rattle in their mind and their being as their reality was shaken up a bit. And some of them began to ponder what it was that they were doing with their lives.

Now, if I was attached to my own *safety*, if I was attached to being *liked*, I would not have allowed that expression of the Holy Spirit to be made manifest. And that is what far too many in your world tend to do:

> *Oh, if I say what just came to my mind, I may not be liked. But I'm really committed to being liked, while pretending to live a spiritual life.*

Therefore, indeed, precious friend, understand well, *you* have no idea what your brother or sister needs—from a gentle kiss on the cheek to a swift kick in the ass. But if you are committed to Love, to innocence, to freedom, to trust, and if you choose to access the perfect freedom of your channel of communion with God, and not to react from the egoic mind, then you will be guided as you need to be. And as you choose to fulfill that purpose, you have fulfilled your own pathway into the depths of knowing God.

So, yes, the Holy Spirit is not a namby-pamby, strawberry jelly kind of energy. The Holy Spirit is committed to one thing: *the Atonement*. The Atonement occurs when illusions are shattered. The Holy Spirit knows what is required. And what is required may not always, shall we say, meet the approval of the social world in which you find yourself. But those afraid to rattle the cages of others are simply afraid. This means they run their life by fear and are more committed to their comfort or safety, which is to be committed to the insanity of the ego, and not to the freedom of Christed Consciousness.

Does that help with that question?

Response: Very much so.

Jeshua: Now, I'm not saying there is not an art involved in that. The degree to which you enact the suggestion of the Holy Spirit comes from your willingness to save not one love for yourself — to be unattached, to recognize that you are the student of the Holy Spirit. You see? Which is, of course, the cultivation of Self-love.

Response: I see.

Jeshua: Indeed. So, have you anything else, or is that sufficient for now?

Response: There are no more questions for this tape, but if you want to continue elaborating on anything, I'm sure we'd all be happy to hear your message.

Jeshua: There is nothing further that we would choose to elaborate upon. We would ask you, however — each and every one listening to this tape: Find some way in which you allow yourself the experience of the *pleasure of Love's presence*. Do not let this day end, from the time you hear this tape until the time you sleep, find a way to enjoy the pleasure of Love's presence. And with that, indeed,

Amen.

Lesson Three

PERSONAL NOTES

The Way of Knowing

PERSONAL NOTES

Lesson Four

Lesson Four

Now, we begin.

And indeed, once again, greetings unto you, beloved and holy friends. Understand well, then, my delight in creating communication devices that allow me to be with *you*. Feel and understand my delight as I seek to look upon the world in which you abide and allow myself to receive the guidance of my Father in how I can best create communication devices that can touch as many hearts and minds as possible.

There is a great advantage to living outside of the realm of the body. I need not spend "time" on the body. And I can see that that strikes some chords among you. The body is not right, and the body is not wrong. The body simply *is*. And in Reality, as you have fallen under the spell of the world that you have created—for no other reason than you wanted to—you have come to perceive the body in a certain way. First of all, you think it is quite solid when, in fact, it is not. You think that the body separates you from others since, as your scientists well know, no two solid objects can occupy the same point of space and time. They're quite right about that.

As you look out, then, through the eyes of the body, you would *actually believe* that you dwell within it, and therefore, have a *private domain* that is all yours. This leads you to the *great delusion* that you can have *private thoughts*. Like one who comes home after a day of work and closes the front door behind them and then rants and raves about their boss or their co-workers, thinking that the walls of the house are around them and that, therefore, they have something called "privacy." Rest assured that this is quite a delusion!

In reality, the body does not contain you. Rather, you contain the body. *Mind* is vast, eternal, and unlimited. *Mind* is what every being that you know participates in, like waves participating in the ocean. This means that anytime you think a thought about anyone, that thought is communicated to them. Now, it's quite true that unless they've done enough work to become sensitive to the subtle levels of Creation, they won't necessarily be aware *consciously* that you are thinking a certain thought about them. They may only be aware that suddenly *they've* had a thought of *you*, and a rather funny feeling is going through their body. And they'll pass it off and give it not a second thought. Likewise, if you think a loving thought, ten thousand miles away someone may suddenly think of you and feel good in their body and not even know why, and just let it go by. Why? Because the belief system says that they must be doing that inside themselves, and it has no connection to you.

In reality, *thought* is the substance of all things. Thought is *an impulse of pure energy*. It is more subtle than anything in the physical domain. Thought travels far faster than the speed of light. In fact, light is actually a *physical occurrence* that emerges long after the birthing of the dream of separation. So while a light year can seem to be quite a vast thing in your world of physics, rest assured that *thought travels instantaneously*. In fact, *thought is immediately present everywhere*. As you are a conscious mind, a body-mind, abiding in the Ocean of Pure Mind, you literally receive the impressions of all thought being thought anywhere. It comes into your auric field. And your auric field is really nothing more than the trough that seems to separate one wave from another — but in fact, the trough of those waves *joins* them one to another.

All fields of thought, then, in a sense, wash up to the shoreline of your being. *You* elect what influences will enter into your sphere. Some of those will pass through, and some you will begin to become identified with. You'll take them on as *your* thought. You'll form an *agreement* with the nature of that thought. You will value that thought, and therefore create

Lesson Four

experiences that flow *from* your agreement, your valuation.

For virtually all beings born within the human sphere, one such agreement is:

> *I am just the body, and therefore I am separate from all others.*

That is merely an agreement, *a decision to create experience*. You are equally free to say within yourself:

> *I am more than a body. My mind is vast and unlimited. And that is the deeper essence of my identity and my existence. I am in perfect communication with all forms of life at all times. I need only withdraw my attention from my perception of my body to access communication with anyone at any time.*

I said once in A Course in Miracles that,

> *You have never forgotten the body, even for a moment. And yet, a moment is all it takes to realize that you are not the body.*

I did not mean by this that you should *deny* the body, but rather, that you be willing to *surrender* your *perception of what the body is*, that it is not a device that separates you at all. And why is this so? You see, you once decided to dream the impossible dream: the dream of separation. The body is the result of that thought—the *attempt* to *create something* that succeeds in separating you from the Mind of God. But you have never succeeded. For in the moment that that began to emerge, the Holy Spirit already translated it into something that is not a *separation* device, but a *communication* device. You failed. The Holy Spirit did not!

This means that the body, itself, is *constantly* receiving input in the form of subtle energy vibration from *everything* and *everyone* around it. You are like a giant radio station that is picking up and transmitting signals constantly. If you would like proof of this, and especially if you would like proof of how powerful thought is as it expresses vibration through the body, simply create what you call in your world, I believe, the *dowsing rods*. Take two pieces of metal. It could be two parts of a coat hanger. Bend them so that you can gently hold one end, and hold them in your hands about six inches from your body. And then have a friend stand about twenty feet away and have them think thoughts of negativity:

> *I am unworthy. I am not worthy of being loved. I have no energy. I'm not worth anything.*

And as they're doing that, walk toward them and see how close you get before your dowsing rods of metal begin to move around. Then, back up and find just the *edge* where their energy field is influencing the rods.

Then go back again, twenty or thirty feet, and have them change their mind. Have them begin to think *loving* thoughts:

> *I am One with God. Love flows through me perfectly. I am so glad to be alive!*

They need not say it out loud. They need not move a muscle. They need only think differently. Then again walk toward them, and see when you find the point where the rods in your hands begin to move about. You'll find that their energy field is *much larger* with the positive thought than with the negative.

Now, your body is like a divining rod. And so is everyone else's. Therefore, those with confidence, those who love themselves, those who are not concerned with the good opinions of the world, who just go forward in the direction of

Lesson Four

what they love, are the ones that seem to gain the greatest support in the Universe. Why? Because when such a one walks into a bank to get a business loan, already knowing that this is a great idea and they're going to bring the fullness of their being to it, and they couldn't possibly fail, just walking in the door, they are bringing an energy field that influences and touches the loan officer.

Those that walk in going:

God, I wish I could get this business loan, but I just don't know. I don't have any experience in this. They're going to look at me like I'm a schmuck.

That person walks in with a much condensed energy field; it's very weak. The quality of vibration of the thought is emanating out and touching the energy field of the loan officer. If you were the loan officer, who would you rather do business with?

Therefore, *Love* ... when *Love* leads the way, when *Love* is the Field of Energy that you are abiding within, everywhere you go, you are touching the Universe in a way much more subtle than the conscious mind. And that Universe will *respond* to you, because Love responds to Itself like a flower that opens to sunlight.

Now, I'm not telling you anything you don't already know. But you haven't stopped to consider how *profoundly important* it is in the nature of your own life. You know that *you* respond to a happy person, to a kind person, to a loving person more than you would to a person who's being wicked. It's simple common sense. You know that you love to be around beings that talk about unlimitedness, that talk about great vision. Why? Because they're reminding you that you, too, are a great visionary, that unlimitedness is the natural state of the

Kingdom of Heaven. The problem is that you've unwittingly taught yourself to live from fear, to think negative thoughts, to believe that the opinions of the world mean something. You have literally created a world in which people are negatively-minded, don't want to support you, don't think you're worth anything. And yet, *you* are the one that's projecting that belief about *yourself*, and you, therefore, will attract a like vibration. For like attracts like.

If you, therefore, want to attract beings who will support you and love you, decide to be a being who supports and loves *yourself*. Decide to open your arms wide, as we spoke of in last month's tape, to receive the Love, the presence, the pleasure of God's Presence. Think only loving thoughts. Learn to master forgiveness. Dare to follow your heart! Celebrate life! Do what brings you joy! Walk as one confident in the Light of Christ! Dare to look out upon the world and say:

> *My Father has set the table before me, and every being and blade of grass is here to support my enjoyment of God!*

And as you cultivate that kind of discipline, *your life will change* — as it *must*. For the Universe responds to the vibrational quality that you are emitting from the radio station of your own mind.

Beloved friends, you are, indeed, Love. But when you decide — as you get up in your day — that you must fear the attitude of the boss, that you must safeguard the feelings of the spouse, that you must sacrifice in order to be conformed to the opinions of the world, you shrink your energy field. And the only thing that leaks out is something like the statement:

> *I choose to live in fear. I'm not willing to be bold and big and happy. I don't want to laugh too much today because somebody*

Lesson Four

might be offended. I won't tell you my truth because it might disrupt your energy field.

All of that is delusion. You are free. You are here to celebrate. You are here to be outrageous. You are here to extend Love, and Love cannot be extended through a contracted energy field. Therefore, teach yourself to notice each fearful thought. Teach yourself to notice when your energy field is contracted and do the opposite: choose to receive Love! And if you start to go through a single day, and you notice that by five o'clock your energy field isn't feeling very good, ask yourself where have you been waiting for Love to show up as a gift of something or someone else to you. Stop what you're doing and be the one who gives Love to yourself — simply so that you can enjoy it.

The essence of this hour's sharing is this: *You, and you alone, are completely responsible for the quality of your experience of each moment.* No one is doing anything to you. The world is not an unsafe place. And what you experience in life is the direct result of what flows from the inside *out*. For there can be no flow from the outside *in*, except that which you *receive* and make *your own*. Is there any point, then, to be fearful of something? Of course not! If you *are* fearful, at least accept that you have *decreed* it to be so:

I choose to be fearful of being a millionaire, and therefore I will not take this opportunity and run with it.

I am fearful of the opinions of others; therefore, I will not give speeches in public.

At least say:

I choose to have the experience of being a contracted and fearful human being.

At least take ownership and recognize the simple Truth that as the world shows up to reflect that fear to you, it is doing so only out of *loving service to you.*

You see, the Universe is only Love. And beings will respond to you according to what you want to call into your being, that's all. Nothing else is even possible. It is quite true that you may be calling a calamity to yourself because you, as a soul, are ready to discover a greater depth of Love and forgiveness in yourself. Life might bring you challenges, but only because you've *asked* it to bring you challenges so that you can grow your capacity to maturely direct Love in this world. Nothing can occur that you have not called to yourself.

I could not begin to tell you how many times I have conspired to create opportunities for many, many beings to step into the fullness of their Christed Consciousness with full power and glory in the shortest possible time, only to have them say,

> *No, no. I can't do that. That's just not who I am. I have to go do something else.*

And the something else is always something based on *fear*, something the egoic part of the mind thinks that they can be comfortable with, and something that will take them *many more lifetimes* to reach the same result.

The Holy Spirit always knows the shortest route to God. It *will*, when presented to you, bring up for you your deepest fears, since it is *fear* that obstructs the Light of Truth. How, then, do you dissolve the power of fear? By recognizing it, by feeling it, and by owning the simple fact that fear is not your master and continuing to walk on. The "ring of fear" of which I speak quite deeply in *A Course in Miracles*, is simply that. The ring of fear is something constructed from the inside out. In Reality, all power

Lesson Four

under Heaven and Earth is given unto the Holy Son of God. And when you are presented with an opportunity, you are not presented something in which you are asked to walk alone. And if you accept the Holy Spirit's function as your own, *every obstacle is removed before you reach it*.

Many would look at this, my beloved brother, and say:

> *Gee, you must really be abiding in Christ Consciousness. Either that, or the Universe has made you special because, no matter what, things always seem to work out and miracles lead the way.*

And yet it is not specialness at all. It is merely his recognition that the Holy Spirit's function is the only *right-minded* function. And that function can look any way it wants to look. He has learned that his delight comes from taking in more of God by surrendering into God.

Shanti Christo is a pebble dropped into the pond of his mind, and into the mind of his friend and, shall we say, cosmic mate, simply because the place was prepared through the cultivation of trust and the decision to follow only that pathway set forth by the Holy Spirit.

Therefore, indeed, beloved friends, where in your life are *you* resisting the opportunities that have been presented to you? Where have you resisted and said,

Well, that's just not me. I'm not that way. I really can't do that,

when, in fact, you're merely afraid of the world? Fear has defeated you. And in *The Way of Knowing*, fear has no power. One simply abides and does, gives it back to God, and goes on.

In the day when your body-mind returns to the dust of the

ground, which is an old way of saying that the energy that is holding the subtle forms of matter (what you call your molecules and atoms) together to create an appearance of something solid . . .When that energy is gone, called the intention and will, the mind is shifted somewhere else and the body dissolves, you will remain as you've always been: pure intelligence, pure potentiality, pure perception. You will still be creating, and you will merely generate energy fields that will create experiences in worlds around you.

You abide, then—*now*—in the perfect opportunity *to walk through* your rings of fear. Therefore, look well. Where do you feel a contraction, a fear, a hesitancy? Is it in something that needs to be said to a friend? The more *transparent* you become, the more you merely speak when you feel moved to speak, do when you feel moved to do, go where you feel moved to go, laugh as you feel moved to laugh, and cry as you feel moved to cry, the less resistance you have to the flow and movement of life emanating from your own heart and soul—recognizing your perfect innocence and the perfection of all things. The more you do that, the more you will create for yourself a mindset, a state of being, so that when the body dissolves and you are in your infinite magnificence, fear will not contract you. You will simply say,

> *Oh! Well! What can I create now? I seem not to have a physical body any more. Hmm . . .How interesting!*

Where you choose to *resist* moving through your rings of fear, *as you know they exist in your current life*, you are building a prison for God's Son—pure and simple. The world will tell you,

> *Do not trust the impulse of the heart.*

Not the impulse of the ego or the mind, but the impulse of the

Lesson Four

heart. And yet, it is in the *heart* that the guidance of the Holy Spirit speaks.

Indeed, beloved friends, in *The Way of Knowing*, there is a *certainty of Knowing* that it is the places in which fear seems to be cropping up that is the actual *doorway* to greater God Consciousness. If there is something that you feel fearful of sharing with another, *there* is your doorway. Go and share your truth, for no other reason—not to persuade, not to be right—but just to do the sharing so that you get through the ring of fear. That's all. If you feel your heart constantly calling you to live as a penniless mendicant on the streets of London, and it's been calling to you for thirty years, go and sell all that you have and *follow your heart*.

Now, I know that the world has not taught you to live in such a way. But the world is the opposite of the Truth of the Kingdom. Love all. Become the one that serves all, by loving first yourself. Learn to quiet the roar and the din of the world, which is nothing more than your decision to place a *value* on how the rest of the world is thinking. Serve only that Voice of Truth within yourself. And that Voice of Truth within yourself is the Voice that says:

> *Boy, go start a garden today! Oh, yes! I don't know how to garden. How am I going to figure this one out? But I really want to start a garden.*

Go start a garden!

Some would say this is living from your *authenticity*. I do not speak of what is authentic as being what the *mind* thinks, that is, its social image. That is not authentic at all. That's a mask, a persona. What is authentic is what you feel in the core and the depth of your being—*in innocence*. And what do I mean by that?

The *innocent heart* is not needy. It doesn't require selected individuals to agree with it. It doesn't wait until the Universe nods its head in approval. It merely *knows* it is innocent and acts from it, and is not attached to the opinions of the world. *Authenticity* is the core through which Christ Mind grows. And any time you look and see that you've not been living authentically, and decide to take a deep breath and let your illusions be shattered by becoming transparent and telling the truth, and allowing whatever changes that need to occur to occur — then indeed, you are growing your Christ Mind.

In *The Way of Knowing*, then, you are asked constantly:

Where am I being inauthentic?

Where am I just showing up the way I think Harry down the street needs me to show up? Where am I being a vegetarian so that I can feel superior to those that are not?

Where am I controlling my diet because I am afraid that this substance will make me less spiritual?

Where am I denying my humanity in order to present an image to another?

Where am I getting up and going to the same job every day, when I know in the secret of my own depth of my beingness, that I just don't want to be there any more?

To live authentically, in some sense, is to live alone. To live alone simply means that you no longer are run by needing to look a certain way, succeed in a certain way, so that the judgment of the world will nod its head and give you a "10" instead of a "1."

Lesson Four

In *The Way of Knowing*, the mind comes to grasp the simple metaphysical Truth that:

> *I, and I alone, am creating my tomorrows. And if I create inauthenticity now, I can rest assured, I will experience it tomorrow. If I create imprisonment for my soul now, I will experience it tomorrow.*

And because Creation is *eternal*, it is impossible not to have a tomorrow — whether in this world or another.

Beloved friends, you were created to create. You were created out of an overflow of Joy and Love. Therefore, live joyously, live lovingly of *yourself*. Dare to consider that your Self is *so important* that you have an obligation never to settle for less than your own authenticity. Sometimes that requires beginning the process of discovering what is authentically yours and not merely the influence of others.

Where, beloved friends, are you still being inauthentic? Where are you responding with a smile when you're actually feeling anger? Where are you responding with an "Okay," when inwardly the answer is, "No"? Where are you responding in fear to a substance you would put in your body?

> *I can't eat that because that's a very bad substance, and I want to be healthy.*

It is the very *fear* that is creating a tomorrow of unhealthiness. Love heals all things. Love transmutes all things. Love embraces all things, and thereby, transcends all things. Where are you not allowing Love to be your Reality?

And so, beloved friends, already in this very short hour, we have spoken to a certain theme, yet again. We ask you to consider it well. Do not be in a hurry to merely put this tape aside. Listen to it a few times. And wherever you suddenly hear a question instead of a statement, pause the tape and spend some time considering it—quietly, as though you were allowing the answer to emerge from your *innocence*. And then ask yourself:

> *What changes can I make so that I'm truly showing up in a more authentic way?*

And with that, we're going to let that be enough for now. For those of you that truly choose to, you'll find that if you abide with the message of this hour, engage the simple quiet questions that are asked, and contemplate certain key thoughts that were, in a sense, repeated, much movement can occur, much liberation can occur.

You are Christ. And you are free in the world of space and time *to know it as deeply as possible.*

And with that, peace be unto you always.

Amen.

Lesson Four

Lesson Four Question and Answer Section

Question: Jeshua, in *A Course in Miracles* you say something about the "Great Rays of Light. "What is that about?

Answer: Indeed, beloved friend, although I did not spend much time in seeking to define it, the Great Rays of Light simply refer to the Truth of each and every one of us. In this way, by way of metaphor, your Creator is as the Central Sun. And out of its overflowing, Rays of Light are cast out. And those Rays of Light are made of one substance with the Light. And yet, something incomprehensible occurs. Each Ray of Light can be seen, in a sense, to stand alone in its relationship to the Central Sun. It is made of the same substance as every Great Ray of Light, and each Ray of Light has its own pure potentiality for the creation of experience. The Great Rays of Light, then, refer to the essence of each and every soul. For the soul is an infinite Ray of Light — eternal, unbounded, unborn, and undying.

But there is another level. And this simply means that the Great Rays of Light is like the realm of ideas. Ideas each carry a certain vibration or quality. The Great Rays of Light are the great ideas, the great visions. For instance, *forgiveness* is a Great Ray of Light. Judgment is a distortion of Light. *Unlimitedness* is a Great Ray of Light. Fear and contraction and limitation are distortions of that Light. You could think of many more: *compassion* instead of control, *trust* instead of fear, and so on.

So Great Rays of Light also refer to the *ideas that liberate the mind*, the ideas that are *eternal* and are found in every form of the Universal Curriculum. Indeed, each and every one of you listening to these words *is* a Great Ray. And the Great Rays have existed *with* that one Central Sun throughout all of eternity. That is the Truth of your being, and it is perhaps the most fundamental Truth that must occur as a Knowingness within the mind:

> *I AM A GREAT RAY OF LIGHT — unbounded, eternal, unborn and undying! Try as I will, I cannot get away from being a creator, a co-creator. So maybe it's time I stopped pretending I am less than a Great Ray, and got on with discovering how I can let that Light shine — even in this world.*

Does that help you in regard to that question?

Response: Yes.

Question: You say that everyone is Christ, yet even among highly enlightened beings, there seems to be some difference. Does everyone have their own *unique soul essence*?

Answer: This is actually a very loaded question. For differences are the effect of perception. That is, ten human beings looking at two enlightened beings might see any number of differences. Some of those differences will be a projection of their own likes and dislikes, and they will, therefore, conclude that one enlightened being is more enlightened than the other enlightened being, which is, of course, a contradiction in terms.

However, it is a great paradox that while Mind is one, while Light is one, Consciousness is one, Awareness is one, Love is one, Creation requires differentiation. In other words, the *creation of relationship*. It is not possible to *know* a thing, to even be aware of a thing, except that you have an awareness that it is not *another thing*. Does that make sense to you? If there was only one thing, that one thing would not even be aware of itself, because it's all there is. You become aware of yourself by knowing how to *distinguish* yourself from a flower. Is that not true? Indeed. Therefore, while you are made of the same

Lesson Four

substance as the flower, there is a *distinction* in the expression of form.

Creation is *extension*. Extension is *expression*. Therefore, each Great Ray of Light, while being of one substance — perfectly the same substance — expresses itself, creation is extended through it, with a *subtle nuance of difference* — a different twist, a different flavor put on it at a very subtle level. And therefore, each being seems to express a unique *individuation*. The *spell*, in the physical dimension of the human mind, is that individuation means separation. It does not. Just as many instruments make up one orchestra that creates its own unique music, so too, do the subtle nuances of differentiation create an orchestration that is called Creation.

Therefore, what is important here is for the mind to realize how much *energy* it spends trying to conform itself to be what it perceives all the other Great Rays are doing. Do you see? *Become your own individuated Ray of Light!* You don't do that by pushing others away. You don't do that by *separating* yourself. You do it by *loving yourself* and following the *impulse* that comes through the depth of a quiet heart.

To own and embrace your individuation and to let your Light shine, so to speak, your authenticity to shine, you actually experience greater *unity* with the Universe than you do by trying to hide your Light under a bushel, and then trying to show up as a personality who pleases everybody else by conforming to the world.

You could say that *I* stood out like a sore thumb. I did not seem to fit in with *anybody*. And yet, my experience was that the more authentically I expressed myself, in the dimension of space and time, *the greater depth of union with my brothers and sisters I experienced. The more honoring and loving of their essence I could be,* the more I could discern their essence, because I was claiming my own essence, my own authenticity. Does that make sense for you?

It's a rather important thing to consider. If you want to *love* in this world, then you had better individuate yourself and love yourself *so uniquely* that you do not conform to anybody else's ideas. You can *agree* with them, in order to play and create, but don't *conform* to them — it's very, very different. Too many human beings suffer because they think their life is shallow. They put all their energy into pleasing everybody else, into showing up in just the right way so they never upset anybody's apple cart. And then they can't understand why their life feels so shallow.

Individuate! Stand out! Shine! Let the power of the Universe move through you. Become the *most unique being anybody's* ever imagined. And when you do that, you will paradoxically feel closer to all of Life than you ever thought possible, for you will be close to your Creator. And when you are close to your Creator, you embrace Creation.

Does that help you in regard to that question?

Response: Yes.

Jeshua: Indeed. Very well. And then, to each and every one of you: I love you, that which is called Shanti Christo. I've said many times that it is designed to express Christ Consciousness and to bring Christ Consciousness to this planet in ways that have not yet been done before. That must mean that it must operate *differently*. So it is, so it shall be!

It will remain to be seen who can *discern* the great differences that are at operation in this adventure. For to *see* the differences will require that that being who sees the differences must have

Lesson Four

changed, in order to see at all. Just something, somewhat cryptic, to consider.

And with that, indeed, beloved friends, be at peace this day. And let your Light shine.

Amen.

PERSONAL NOTES

Lesson Four

PERSONAL NOTES

The Way of Knowing

PERSONAL NOTES

Lesson Five

Lesson Five

Now, we begin.

Once again, beloved friends, we join together with you because we remain as committed as you are to discovering ever greater depths of God's presence, ever greater depths of our own presence, ever greater depths of what alone is true always, of what alone is unchanged, unchanging, and unchangeable, forever.

Indeed, beloved friends, we would speak unto you in this hour of that which deepens the understanding of abiding in Perfect Knowing, in Perfect Knowledge. We want to address for you a theme that you have heard before, though from a slightly different perspective. That theme goes by a term that most of you are familiar with, and that term is "karma." Karma, as popularly considered, means that for every action there is an equal and opposite reaction. For everything you put out, a similar energy returns.

Now, I have said before that karma can exist only where unconditional loving does not. This means that to the degree that your mind has not been purified of *fear*, that the mind has not been purified of *need*, that the mind has not been purified of its tendency toward *idolatry*—that is, creating something which is a substitute for Love, mistaking form for content—wherever this is occurring you are, indeed, experiencing the creation of karma. What do we mean by that? Each time you hold an unloving thought, you are going to experience the effect or the fruit of that thought. In reality, there are two levels at which this occurs, or two ways in which it occurs. The first is immediate. The second is mediated through the forms of time.

In the first, in that which is immediate, the very moment you think an unloving thought, as you are as a physically-embodied being, you immediately alter the electrical flow of energy throughout the physical system. You immediately alter the chemical balance of the body and, thereby, experience tightness in the body, sadness perhaps, depression, an overall ill-at-ease feeling. For every negative thought, not just the big ones that you really get your attention wrapped about, but even the small ones, this is still true. Depression can only occur in a mind that has been denying its pathway to joy.

Depression, then, is the result of a *resistance* to the true flow of Life throughout the body-mind. This resistance occurs in many ways. It can result as the result of not feeling a feeling to its completion, withholding a simple truth, and — more often than not — from denying the impulse of the heart. And as you begin to walk a spiritual path, and realize you need to be open to the guidance of the Holy Spirit — that, in fact, you cannot awaken yourself, because if you could you would have already done so — and then the opportunities are *presented* that contain within them *all* that you need to awaken from your illusions . . . but you resist it because it doesn't conform to your image of yourself.

So, you see, there are many ways in which you can resist and create a blockage in the flow of energy through the system. It is all around some form of a negative thought. And all negativity is an expression of fear. All attempt to control another is really fear. Anger is merely a form of fear. So, the very moment in which the mind is used to think a negative thought, there is a very immediate karmic effect. Given that effect over a period of time, an illness is created in the body, depression is created in the emotional field.

Now secondly, there is a *mediated* form of karmic response — namely, that the world around you will, over a period of time, coagulate, create itself in a context that will *mirror* to you that which seems to *prove* the negative thought that by now you have forgotten you even created. And then you will have the negative thought again and you will mistakenly believe that the negative thought is there *because of* the conditions outside of you.

An example would be for someone to see an event occur in life, such as the government raising taxes, and then say,

> *Yup, I've always known that that's the way it is. You cannot trust a single politician.*

And yet, that one is not seeing that fifteen years ago, he decided that politicians could not be trusted because he heard it from his father and "knows," in the sense of his mind, that the politicians will always do something to take more money out of his pocket. Then fifteen years later, when taxes are raised, the mind says,

> *I knew it. I think I must have been right all along. See what they did? This means that politicians can't be trusted.*

When in fact, the politicians are merely the manifestation that *fulfills* the *prophecy*.

In this way, I want to invite you to look at your life. How are the events that are occurring, the quality of life you are living, how could they possibly be reflecting a self-fulfilling prophecy? Or how, in other words, could it be merely the fulfillment of the *karma* of how you are using the mind?

Usually, in this secondary form of the way karma shows up, the beliefs or thoughts are very, very *old*, deep in what you call your unconscious. In fact, as you go back in time and look at your life, ask,

What must I have believed previously for this effect to be showing up?

For instance, if it is regarding money—if you have no money, look well at what you have *believed* about money in the past. Especially look to see,

What were the beliefs about money that my parents held?

For indeed, as we have touched on before, each soul drops, in a sense, into this world through the *context* of the parents. There is a context of perception, belief, and attitude that you begin to be *colored* by because you are accepting that coloration into the field of your own energy, as a means of making contact with this world and emerging into it. If, for instance, the parents believe that spirituality and material wealth cannot go together and, therefore, to be spiritual means to do without, materially, then look at how your life has evolved. Do you find a block at receiving moneys for being of service to others, but no block in receiving money for doing something you dislike?

Live in that question, beloved friends, and begin to apply it to the whole of your life. Begin to look at your life, look at the affects you experience as your surroundings and your context. Are you alone, with no lover or friends, hmm? What have you believed about the world previously? For somewhere, it is the nature of your thought, the agreements you've made unconsciously or consciously about what things mean, the agreements you have made with the culture in which you have been birthed, the family into which you have been birthed, that has actually generated the energy that is showing up as the *affects* you experience as your life. What thoughts or beliefs were you holding within the mind?

One common thought might be,

Lesson Five

Oh, I just can't really make it on my own. I need to be taken care of. I don't believe I have what it takes.

Then, twenty-five years later, you wonder why you feel resentment toward the mate. The resentment is merely the recognition that you thought a negative thought about *yourself*, acted upon it, and have created the effects of someone who is controlling and provides you with all your money. You think there is a fault in *them* because you have forgotten to see the pebble that you dropped into the pond of omnipotent creativity which *is* the domain of the mind.

Karma, then, is an *effect* of how the mind is used.

Now, I have, indeed, said that karma can only exist where unconditional loving does not. What does this mean? When the mind *unconditionally loves*, it loves first *itself* and places *no conditions* upon what it *receives* as ideas from the universe.

There are many in your world that look up to those who take the greatest chances in life—the actor or the actress who waits on tables at some cheap hamburger stand, sleeps on a park bench, keeps taking acting classes and, finally, gets the part and becomes rich and famous. And yet, that one who became rich and famous is one who received the impulse of a desire to act, and followed up on it, and was willing to do whatever it took to be in the contexts in which something may or may not occur—the *willingness* to take the risk. Such a one is living, actually, in a state of unconditional Love of the self. And whether they think about it or not, they are carrying the subtle belief that the universe will somehow arrange itself and will support them to follow their heart.

In *unconditional loving*, karma does not exist. The example I have given you is just a rudimentary phase of unconditional loving. In its *mature* state, in its *spiritual* state, unconditional loving means that the mind has awakened and seen that nothing that occurs in life can *cause* it to contain or withdraw its Love. In the perfection of Unconditional Love, the mind simply loves. Karma, then, cannot be said to *exist*, because that mind is no longer experiencing *effects* coming back at it. It has *transcended* the world of cause and effect and, regardless of what arises, it merely loves. And who can be imprisoned who simply loves?

So there is a *transcendence* of karma through *Unconditional Love*. And Unconditional Love is always the fruit of the decision to love *oneself*—not because it's a duty to do so, not because it will make your husband love you more. You love yourself because you finally recognize that you might as well. That's all. You love the Self because your Creator loved you enough to create the Self.

There truly are no effects that are occurring as the result of a source of power outside of you. In other words, nothing is being done *to* you. Nothing. And you are free, in each and every moment, through the Power of Love, to free yourself of what *looks like* the effects of the world. In Truth, you are never at the effect of anything but the illusions of thought and belief that you have learned to project *onto* the world.

Many of you feel somewhat fearful of telling your friends and neighbors that you listen to tapes in which a human being is channeling the guidance of Jesus, or Jeshua. That very *fear* that you feel, that constriction, is *karmic*. Somewhere a long time ago, you decided that following your own pathway must stay concealed and isn't worth very much—that nobody will agree, and that *their opinions decide your worth*.

I would ask you this question:

Lesson Five

Could there be fear in simply sharing with your friends that you listen to channeled tapes of Jesus of Nazareth? Could there be fear of sharing that, if there was no prior belief that the opinions of others have the power to decide whether you are good or bad, worthy or unworthy?

If that was not in place, there could not be the fear. So, somewhere you have believed that there is a world outside of you whose opinions matter. Where, then, in your life do you limit your expression of your joy and your fun of simply being alive because you are concerned about the approval of others?

Karma is a most interesting concept and it shows up in many, many ways.

Where are the effects I experience in my life the result of karmically-induced thought, as opposed to thoughts of unconditional self-acceptance?

Beloved friends, the fact that you are experiencing yourself as a body-mind is, in many ways, karmic. That is, it is the result of the vast expanse of mind to dare to think a tiny, mad idea — and take it seriously — that I could separate myself from the Love of God and create an experience that *convinces* me that I have *succeeded* at achieving separation.

And yet, Unconditional Love transforms the experience of the body into something quite different. Unconditional Love of Self translates the life of the body-mind — the life of paying taxes, the life of keeping your car well oiled . . . all of it is translated so that the world becomes not something that proves your unworthiness, your separation, but rather, as a medium of communication in which magic, in a sense, is always at play, miracle-mindedness is always at play.

You go to take your car to fill up your gas tank. Because your heart is open, your mind is open, you are not in resistance to it, your eyes are open—you look around you and you feel the energy of somebody at the pump on the other side of the island (I believe they call it an island. I do not know how they can call it an island. There is no water around the concrete.) However, on the other side of the island you feel the energy of someone and because your heart is open, you go up to them and say,

Oh, I'm just here pumping my gas. I looked up and saw you. You've got a great smile. You've made my whole day. Thank you!

And then, a conversation is struck and it is discovered that they are looking for someone in their corporation who happens to have your skills. And you're looking for a new job.

The things of the world become translated into that which supports your ever- increasing joy, success, fun, pleasure, material improvement, new friends. It supports all of it when you see through the Eyes of Love. When you literally look at the world around you and finally get that it was never what you thought it was, because you failed to separate yourself from God. And *everything* you see is there to support *your happy experience*. You are free to live in your highest joy, to ask for what you want, to open the heart and love—and the universe will respond *according* to the beliefs you hold about yourself, within yourself.

Look at your life, then, as indeed your karma: action that is occurring in response to a former action. One of the most powerful things you could ever do is to ask the question,

> *What must I have believed is true about the world to be living the life I am living now?*

Lesson Five

This is not to say that karma is wrong or bad. It is not. It is merely effect—cause and effect:

> *Where in the effects I'm experiencing now can I bring a greater degree of unconditional, loving acceptance?*
>
> *Where am I looking through the eyes of boredom instead of appreciation? Where can I bring a greater depth of Unconditional Love?*
>
> *Where can I let go of resistance?*
>
> *Where can I give up trying to direct my own life and allow the Love of God to direct my life?*

Karma can be transcended by *translating it* into something else. Karma can become the fulfillment of your purpose, your very way to extend and teach only Love. For when you see that the effects, called your life, are the result of limited or fearful or negative thoughts or beliefs you have held about yourself and about the world, you can embrace the effects you've created and see them in a new light:

> *I choose to allow these very conditions to be those conditions under which I now learn to choose Love.*
>
> *What can I appreciate in this moment?*
>
> *What can I give forgiveness unto?*
>
> *Where can I overcome fear of speaking out and share a truth with a friend?*
>
> *What have I been avoiding that I can now embrace?*

In that very means, any set of conditions, created as the effect of fear-based thinking, now becomes the very *pathway* that will lead you to *transcend* the negative thinking and enter a domain of the use of the mind that will create effects far more enjoyable, far more expansive, than you've ever imagined.

Do not, then, lament your life as it is, for it is *absolutely perfect*. And each set of conditions contains within itself everything you need to translate your life into that which expresses your love of God. Never lament what you create. Never lament what you experience. Never judge yourself and say,

> *Oh, why did I do that? I should have done this other thing.*

No. Appreciate what you have created. Find what can be appreciated within it. Wrap the arms of your Love around it. Bring Unconditional Love to it. And thereby, you will find a window, a doorway, the creation of a new use of the mind that must necessarily *require* the Universe to *rearrange* Itself to accommodate the new vibration. Appreciation and Love and unlimitedness *require* the Universe to show up in a different way.

Karma is not your prison, in other words. Bringing your *attention* to the affects you create is a pathway to great freedom. What you did in the past to create the effects that you no longer want was not a sin or a mistake. It was merely a free choice in order to create experience. Okay, you've been there, you've done that. Now, bring Love and appreciation to the very effects that you may be judging:

> *Why did I buy that stock? It was so silly. I didn't get enough information and now the company has gone bankrupt and I just lost ten thousand dollars. Ah-h-h, let me be in appreciation of this very effect. Yes. Well, this is fantastic! I create experience for myself. I can do more of this. This is great! Oh, I just love myself*

Lesson Five

so much! I can decide. Oh, this is great! I just learned a valuable lesson. Next time I'll get more information. Ah, I'd like another opportunity for a great stock opportunity to make money. Ah, yes! Oh, I'm going to be an expert at this — I can see it coming — through my Unconditional Love. Yes, yes!

In fact, every time you think you've failed, *celebrate!* Celebrate your so-called failure as though it were a success. For remember, it is up to *you* to decide what you will perceive. Events are just neutral. Therefore, you are free to celebrate what you *call* your failures. And when you celebrate them, they are your successes. Any successful person knows that they never *fail*. They merely *learn* and become wiser.

Become one, then, who is no longer at the effect of karma. But rather, become one who uses karma *wisely* by looking honestly at their life, learning what needs to be learned — without judgment, but rather in *celebration*. Become one who translates their karma into the doorway to an ever-increasing awareness of God's Presence and Perfect Love — spread across the face of the Earth, permeating everything you see, translating the world into the very means that can uplift you, awaken you, care for you and heal you.

And so, beloved friends, again we ask that you listen well to the *theme* of this hour, to the *questions* that have been given unto you, that you *spend time with them*. For you see, in *The Way of Knowing*, the mind that abides in a perfectly liberated state *knows* that the world of effects that that mind is experiencing contain within them the very secrets to an ever-increasing delight in the presence of God's Love, that there is no such thing as failure. There is only ongoing success, as Life evolves from good, to better, to best — as the mind learns to be the Presence of Love.

Freedom is Love under all conditions.

And with that, peace be unto you always.

Amen.

Lesson Five

PERSONAL NOTES

The Way of Knowing

PERSONAL NOTES

Lesson Six

Lesson Six

Now, we begin.

And indeed, once again, greetings unto you, beloved and holy friends. As always, I come forth to abide with you as *merely* your brother and your friend. Remember, always, that a brother, or a sister, is not someone who is above you, but who is your equal. Remember, always, that a friend is one who has chosen deliberately to see in you the perfection of Christ, and all greatness that can be birthed through you, until you are willing to see yourself in such a Light. And then, that friend joins with you in holy relationship — to create, to play, to extend the Truth of Reality.

For you were born and created to *create* and not to *make*. What, then, is the difference between *making* and *creating*?

Making requires the special efforts of the egoic mind. Making involves planning what one *wants* based on what one *already knows*, and then setting about to find the way to bring it into being according to one's own ideas. Making always has an element of fear, since the ego itself *is* the fundamental contraction of fear.

Creating, in the way that I'm using these terms, is quite different. When I say that you were born to create, you were created to create, I mean that being made in the Creator's image your only function is to serve as a conduit through which the unfathomable mystery and beauty of Love can be expressed in ways that can be *seen* in this world. An artist can do that with a brush, a singer with a song, a writer with a word, a friend with a smile, a gardener with a garden. You are *in* the act of extending creation whenever you surrender your own ideas of what a thing is or is for, and choose only to do what you do in order to enjoy the presence of Love and the offering of that Love to whomever or whatever will receive it.

Creation, then, is the process in which the creator extends herself/himself from the world of the formless into the world of form. When you choose to invite friends to dinner, and have no ulterior agenda except to be with them and to create a good salad and some soup for them—just because you love them, because you are in a joyful state of being—you are extending the Presence and Reality of God. Surely, this is much different than what your politicians do when they invite friends for dinner. Therefore, indeed, beloved friends, they are involved in *making*, while your dinner is the *flow of creation*.

In the flow of creation, the *form*, itself, is always recognized to be *secondary*; it is a mere instrumentation for the *content*. In *making*, the *form* becomes *very important*. And why? Because in making, the egoic mind already believes it knows what things are and what they are for, since all things are for the ego's safety and continuance. And therefore, the form of how things are done becomes *very* important, for form is image and not content. In creation, the form is as you most desire it to be because it gives you *joy*, not because you believe it will coerce someone else into voting for your party.

Imagine, then, if those of your actors and actresses were more interested in wearing clothing for their great Oscar nominations that brought them joy, as opposed to seeing how good they could look, what will be acceptable, what will be breathtaking, what will grab the attention of others. Rest assured, many of them would show up in their pajamas. Hmm!

The difference between making and creating is the difference between illusion and Reality. Reality *is* the Love which is God. It is the Creator's Will to extend Love. You were created out of the Will of the Creator—and therefore, *your will* to express Love is the *Will of God*; they are one and the same.

Lesson Six

The egoic mind, around the subject of Love since we're on it, is interested in *making* love. It has very set ideas of what Love should *look like*, what *form* it should take, how other beings ought to *respond*, what actions are okay and what aren't okay. But in creation, Love merely extends Itself with *innocence*. When your will is one with your Creator, you are not in the least bit interested in *making* love. You are only interested in *celebrating* the Reality that you are already *in* Love, and you are already *as* the expression of Love. You are innocent and you are perfect, just as you are. The form of that expression becomes quite secondary, since it is merely a temporary instrumentation for the fulfillment of the heart's desire to celebrate the Reality of *being in Love*.

Let me, then, ask you this question: In your own life, do you exert energy in trying to *make* Love happen, or do you celebrate that you are already in the *presence* of Love? For in the former, you must coerce other beings to join your making, and then try to persuade them of how they ought to be behaving, performing, accepting, receiving—so that you feel you've succeeded in manifesting what you've already determined in the mind. *Making love* requires others. *Creating Love*, that is, extending Love, requires nothing but your will, your willingness. This means that you are perfectly free and do not require—do not *need* – the world to show up in any certain *form* before you decide to be *in* Love. And when you are *in* Love, *Love will guide the expression of form.*

That's truly how simple it is. And you will know right away if a smile is enough, whether to another human being or to a leaf on a tree. You'll know, if you're with another, exactly how to express it. There won't be a question, there won't be a doubt. There will be no interference of the egoic mind. There will be no fear. For when the mind is truly in the Will of God, there is no time. Since there is no time, there is no reference to the past, and no reference to the future. For these things abide in the duality of time. They are not part of what alone is eternal. The past has passed away. The future is, at best, a fantasy in the mind. The *present* is where God abides.

The Peace of Christ, then, depends on your willingness to abide in the present for no other reason than to extend creation, to be one who receives Love, acknowledges the presence of Love, breathes Love, and then allows It to flow through the body-mind, through the voice, through the handwritten word, through the wink of an eye — whatever it is — and then you're done with it and you're on to the next moment. The Peace of Christ comes only to that mind that withdraws valuation from the past and the future, and surrenders into the present. For only in the present can Love be *felt, known,* and *extended.* Such a mind *is* a creator. And through that mind, the perfection of Love's extension flows — without impediment, without obstacle, and without mistake.

The mind, then, that is free, free from the egoic need to make, to control, to shape, the mind that is free from identification with the past and anxiety over the future, abides in the perfectly eternal *now* — for no other reason than to receive the awareness that it abides in Love's perfect presence, and then allows that mysterious Reality through that mind, right where it is, *as* it is. It doesn't need to make a show. This isn't about having a prescribed set of activities to do. You are merely present in the moment, and *Love lives you.*

Holy relationship, then, is where any two beings choose to come together and simply each of them, individually, chooses to be *in* the presence of Love. And then, whatever happens, happens. Perhaps one will sit in a chair and read a book while another one watches a movie. Perhaps they will come together and create a beautiful dinner. It really becomes quite irrelevant, because they will be moved by the mysterious energy of Love, Itself, which is the Will of God creating experience *through* His Creations. And when that moment is gone, it's gone. And the mind of each of them simply finds itself in a new present moment.

The difference between *making* and *creating* is essential in *The Way of Knowing*. Therefore, I want to invite you, in this hour's theme and message, to begin to look at your own life. Where are you resting in Knowing and allowing Creation to flow through you in each present moment, and where does your mind become absorbed in what you think you must *make* occur? Come to discern the difference between the two, and notice the quality of *feeling* that is within you when you are in each of those states.

If you are diligent, you will come to see that whenever you are in the mode of *making* love, *making* life conform to what you *think* it ought to be, you are in suffering. When you are *creating*, you are enjoying the miracle of Creation, Itself. For you are in a very unique position. You are both That One through whom Creation flows, and you are also the witness of, or the observer of, the act of Creation flowing from the Mind and Heart of that Creative Center I have called *Abba*, Who is but Love.

Celebrate, then, and embrace the uniqueness of yourself as the Son of God. You are one who gets to *experience* Love, *create* Love, and also observe and witness the *flow* of Love. And if you do not understand that that is *miraculous*, then spend as much time as you need to alone, without moving a muscle, until you get it. For that is the Truth of your Reality. It is timeless and eternal, and far transcends the boundaries of the physical body and the boundaries of your *ideas* about your physical self—your personality, your personal history, your children, your mates, your bank accounts. It far transcends everything that is temporarily arising in the field of form.

As the Holy Son of God, as that created Spirit, birthed to create, your ability to be aware of the flow of Love is unborn and undying — you will never lose it. As the Holy Son of God, the power of your ability, the power of your beingness to allow Love to flow through you is unlimited forever, and it will never be taken away. As the Holy Son of God, your capacity to enjoy the very act of being the One through whom Love is extended is without equal in all of Creation, and it, too, is never taken from you.

Those three aspects are really one thing. And they are the Truth of who you are. And any time your mind has fallen under the power of the egoic mind, which is just to choose wrongly and insanely for a moment, the Reality of your being never goes away. It's never changed or altered in any way. All that has occurred is that you have used time to *lose* awareness of the Truth. And in the next moment, you are free to choose again. The Healed Mind is One which accepts Its True Knowingness:

> *I and my Father are One. Only Love is real. I cannot possibly be a victim of what I see, since what I see is what I choose to see. And if I choose to see with the Eyes of Love, all I see is perfect innocence and the Will of my Father clearly at work.*

The Healed Mind is simply One that rests in that simple Reality. It has merely trained Itself to always choose for the Voice for Love, that's all. It doesn't matter what arises and passes away. The Healed Mind is *not* a mind that can *make* whatever It wants to happen, happen. That is the egoic attempt to become absolutely powerful. The meek of heart — the pure of heart — are those who realize that *making* is the illusion. *Being* is the reality.

Making and creating — *doing* frantically or *being* the presence of

Lesson Six

Love, out of which creative contexts emerge because it is the Will of the Creator to extend Himself through a myriad of forms that arise and pass away. The forms change, but the content or the essence does not. And the Awakened Mind is awakened to the ever-present flow of content, pervading all form, at all time. This is why, for the Awakened Mind, loss is not possible, and death is seen as unreal. For death can pertain only to the *form*. Forms begin in time and end in time, such as a body; that is a form you're very clearly aware of. Ideas have a beginning and an end. Love is the only thing that knows neither beginning nor end, being the fundamental energy of God Itself.

The Healed Mind does not plan. What does that mean? It doesn't mean that it doesn't structure a day — that is, make decisions whether its going to make this phone call now and that one later. But it does not plan what the day shall be *for*. It merely surrenders into Love and allows *Love* to *birth* the day. Do you see the difference? The egoic mind arises in the morning already believing it knows what this one day is for, and this day can have no purpose but the sustaining of the authority of the ego and trying again to make the world conform to what the egoic mind believes must be so. The Awakened Mind knows that this day has no purpose, save that which the Creator would give to it — through the Mind, through the Self. And so, It seeks first the Kingdom and then all things are added unto It. The day flows *out of* Its surrender to Love.

The Healed Mind — the *truly Healed Mind* — is One who is like the wind. When you look upon the wind, you cannot tell from where it's coming, and you don't know where it's going. It's not a logical thing; *you* can't control it. You can see its effects. You can try to measure it. You might even try to predict it. But it will always leave you guessing.

A Healed Mind is not interested in *making*. Its only interest is the delight and joy of *creating*. It merely shows up where it is asked to be. It no more laments or complains if it is asked to work twenty-three hours a day at bringing forth some creation that extends the Presence and Love of God. It merely does what is asked. The Healed Mind is no longer attached to the world's definitions of success or failure. For those pertain to the realm of *making*. It is no longer attached to what others *think* of Its creation, for It trusts the Mystery that has birthed It and that operates through It in each moment.

Indeed, beloved friends, consider well: are you devoted to *making* or *creating*? By way of a simple exercise, in this very moment, how are you approaching the listening to this tape? Did you remember to begin it, as we've suggested many times, as one who knows that they are already Christ and they are merely sitting down to abide with a brother and a friend who is their equal and sees the Truth of them? To open the heart and trust that what emerges in the form of your experience, as you listen to these words, is exactly what is perfect for you in this moment? Or did you sit down determined to make yourself like Jeshua by *memorizing the words*, by *getting the concept*?

The relaxed mind absorbs all knowledge. The making mind misses all knowledge. The relaxed and healed mind is like a sponge that is constantly learning and being shaped by what it learns. The making mind has no room in it to receive anything new because it has already decided what the truth is, what it should look like, and what it should sound like. It misses the moment in which it can observe, be the conduit for, and the one who is creating, an experience of Love.

In this moment, then, you are quite free to truly open the heart and relax the mind and to realize you are present with a brother, and together you are *in* the Field of Love. And all that arises, arises in Mystery and returns to its Source. If you can enter into such a Field of Mind, in this very moment you are free. And you are, indeed, One who Knows. If you can join with me in such a Mind — in this very moment then you can prove to yourself how infinitely powerful you are. And what you can apply to *this* moment can be applied to all moments.

Likewise, if your mind is currently insisting that you cannot be That One in this moment, you're doing the very same thing. You're using the infinite power of the mind to choose to remain a *maker*, and therefore, to reside in suffering. Either way, you remain quite right. Either way, you are expressing your infinite and perfect freedom — to *create* or to *make*, to be in Love or to be in fear, to abide in peace or to abide in anxiety.

Now, ask within yourself,

> *Would I choose to experience what is unending — myself — as a creator or a maker?*

If you choose the path of the creator, then the first thing you need to do is to remember that creating is not the same as making. Creating involves seeking first the Kingdom of Heaven. Now what does that mean? Well, it means that you have to sell all that you own, get a backpack, buy a ticket to Kathmandu, and spend seventeen years hiking through the Himalayan Mountains until you find just the right cave, and then another seventeen years of astute meditation and prayer before you begin to get your first glimpse of God. That is what seeking the Kingdom involves. Or, you can simply turn the mind to the Peace of God — right where you are — and accept it. And in that very moment, you will have gained what all the yogis in their caves have ever gained, what all of the Buddhas and Christs have achieved in their austerities. The Kingdom is but a choice away:

The Way of Knowing

I choose now for the Perfect Peace of God.

And just like that, you've achieved all that needs to be achieved — *if* you receive it.

To create means that you are committed to seeking first the Kingdom of Heaven, then allowing yourself to celebrate that, regardless of what your physical eyes show you, regardless of how the brain-mind is interpreting or creating perception of what the physical eyes reveal to it, regardless of all of that, *you are free*. For whatever is arising is perfectly harmless. Forms come and go, Love remains. And where else can you possibly find freedom, except as one who is merely abiding as the decision for Love?

If you would be a creator, you'll need to give up *striving*, for striving is part of the world of making. And you will need to give yourself permission to cultivate a mastery of *allowing*. Allowing is not a passivity. Allowing is not sitting on your pillow waiting for the Universe to manifest good things in your life. Allowing is an act of turning within, appreciating your Oneness with God, and simply asking,

Father, what would you like to create in this moment?

And suddenly, a thought comes. And the thought reveals you driving your car thirty-five miles to see a friend and inviting them to dinner. Well, then, get on with it! Driving your car for thirty-five miles is an act that takes energy. It is not a passive act at all. *Allowing* is a very powerful state of being, for allowing does not resist anything in the field of action — anything! And if you are asked to create a retreat center in northern New Mexico, well, you simply get on with it, even though you have no idea how it's going to come to pass. You merely make yourself available and you show up.

Lesson Six

On the outside, then, a creator — a true creator — may look very ordinary. A creator may look to be one who is, shall we say, not getting the applause of the world. Their picture may not be on the front of what you call the *People* magazine. Hmm! They may not be the centerfold in the *Playboy* or *Playgirl*. A creator is one who is delighting in allowing the flow of Life to find ways to touch hearts and minds with Love. The creator is not about storing up golden coins for a winter's day. The creator is merely about watching, being a conduit for, and being involved in, the creative extension of Love. That creation might require the storing up of golden coins, for the creator resists nothing of the world. Nothing is seen as good or bad, it's just an instrumentation for effecting the Will of God. And the Will of God is the extension of Love. And when you are involved in *that*, your will is one with the Father, that's all.

The difference between *making* and *creating* is essential in *The Way of Knowing*. It would behoove you, then, to spend some time, over the next month or so, in merely abiding in the innocence of observing your life and beginning to notice when your energy gets caught up with *making* instead of *creating*. Where have you, perhaps, given your life over to making, wishing you could create? Begin to observe the moments in your day when you can choose to create, and remembering that to choose to create means:

> *I give this moment over for the Will of my Father. I wonder how I could simply surrender into being the presence of one who has accepted the Kingdom for him or herself? And then I'll see where it carries me in the next second.*

So that you begin to see that regardless of what is arising in the conditions around you, or what other minds are doing in this world . . . I've said that this world is a big clash of dreams, and the vast majority of minds are still far more committed to illusion than Reality ... to come to see that the world has no effect on you. There are just events arising and passing away. And in any context, your mind remains free to give up making for creating, and then surrendering that moment to the Will of God.

Accepting the Atonement for yourself is another way of saying accepting Love's presence—breathing it in and celebrating it:

Ah, yes! This is all that's really real anyway. Ah-h-h. I wonder what would want to be created in this moment?

And then observing the delightful expression of that *Will* in that moment, that's all. When I said,

The meek shall inherit the Earth,

it means that eventually there will be established as the pervasive quality of human consciousness just this state of being. The world will be populated by creators who arise in the morning going:

The day really belongs to the Creator. I'm just created to extend the Creator's Will.

Father, what would be a groovy way to hang out this day?

Some of those minds might hear,

Oh, just hang out in the forest and listen to the birds.

And so, those beings will give their day to delighting as deeply as possible in the experience of the singing of the birds. Others will hear a different message. And they will set about and do whatever they are asked. Why? Because the mind of the creator

Lesson Six

is no longer in resistance. Sanity has been re-established and there's nothing to fret about.

The mind involved in *making* listens for the impulse of God, and then has a million reasons why that *cannot be*. And those reasons are *always* linked to learning that has occurred in the *past* or anxiety about an imagined *future*. In other words, the mind of a maker is *never present*. It is caught up in the illusion of duality, not the Reality of Perfect Oneness.

One who Knows is a creator. And a creator is empty of himself, that is, empty of the self that was made in error. The Knower of Reality is the presence of Love, the spaciousness through which the Creator extends Its Perfect Will. It has no attachments and no illusions. It is not run by what other people think of It. It is not run by what It has accomplished in the past, or what It perceives It must have in the future.

The mind of one who Knows and rests in true creativity is merely present, witnessing the *extraordinary*, mysterious ways of Love. For Love allows all things, embraces all things, trusts all things, and therefore, transcends all things. And perfect peace can only exist where the mind has *transcended* all conflicted states of duality. Transcendence is not denial. It can come only through embracing, through allowing, through being present.

Your mind is a mind that *has* been healed. You do not need to heal it. You only need to accept that healing has been accomplished by the grace of that Love that birthed you to create. That is what I meant when I have said a teacher of God need only accept the Atonement for themselves.

I am already healed. Time to get on with it.

All forms of healing, then, are merely contexts created by Love through a mind that has accepted healing—a context created that would give the mind that perceives itself as unhealed an opportunity to choose differently.

Therefore, I want to create for you a context in this very moment. A way of demonstrating to you exactly what I've been sharing with you in this hour. For in this moment, as a brother and friend who loves you, and loves my Father, I am merely allowing myself to create words recorded on a tape that helps to create a context that I am literally observing emerge. I have not planned it. I'm not trying to make anything happen. I am abiding in Love.

And out of that Love I am now receiving the thought from the Will of my Father. I am observing it flow through my mind into the field of being that you would know as this, my beloved brother, being translated through electrical impulses into that which creates a vibration of vocal cords, that creates words that are recorded onto a tape, that are then heard by your ears, that send vibrations to your brain-mind—and giving you permission to access it with the deeper Self that Knows the Truth.

I am witnessing all these things even as it flows through my mind toward yours.

I invite you, then now, into the context of healing. Say, then, this within your holy mind:

> *My mind has already been healed by the Grace that birthed me in Its image. I need only use the power of that mind to choose the perfect Peace of God. I do so now and forevermore. I am one who Knows.*

Lesson Six

Father, what would You create in this moment that is an extension of Love?

And do nothing but observe what comes into your mind — what feeling suddenly flows through the body.

There! Short exercise. A context to demonstrate how it all works. No magic, no pilgrimages, no special pills, no special diet, no special love affairs — nothing *special* at all. Simply the presence of Mind. And rest assured, in that moment, if you were truly joining with it, you had no thought whatsoever that you are a separate ego who does not know God. You were that Mind enjoined in the creative process itself. You were in your *right-mindedness*. And in that moment, you are the Knower. And as a Knower, you are free to have as many moments of that Knowing as *you* want to experience.

So, beloved friends, merely observe the mind for a while, until you learn to detect the difference between making and creating. You'll come to discover that creating is much more fun, takes a lot less energy or effort, and creates a whole lot more joy within your own experience, your own energy field. Delight in that simple practice, and remember: you don't have to go to a temple in Tibet to perfect it. For wherever you are, you are in the Temple created for you by the Creator who loves you and knows exactly how to enlighten, forevermore, the Mind of the Creator that He has created. Enjoy creating!

And with that, indeed, beloved friends, peace be unto you always, you who are eternally perfect Co-creators with our Father. Peace be unto you always.

Amen.

The Way of Knowing

Lesson Six Question and Answer Section

Question: What is the difference between *joy* and *pleasure*, and why do a lot of spiritual traditions denounce pleasure?

Answer: It is a very wise question you've been prompted to ask in your willingness to be a creator. Hmm! There is, indeed, a difference between *joy* and *pleasure*. In your human realm, in the realm of the body-mind, joy and pleasure are often deeply confused. And so the mind becomes hoodwinked into pursuing *pleasure*, believing it will find *joy*.

How, then, to distinguish between the two?

Pleasure is dependent on a specific energetic state temporarily passing through the nervous system of the body. Joy is a quality of recognition in the Spirit, or the Deep Mind, or the Heart, that *transcends* all conditions. A mind that is awake can know joy in the midst of what appears to be the hardships that can pass by in life.

By way of my own experience as a man upon your plane, your world would say that my crucifixion was a *very* painful experience. There was a lot going on in the body, but I was in a state of joy, not a state of pleasure. When I danced and sang and drank some wine and broke bread with my friends, I experienced pleasure. That is, the food substances, the vibrations of the music, created a temporary pattern of energy in the nervous system that elicited certain reactions within the brain-mind and the body itself—pleasurable sensations.

I learned, because I was taught to learn, that pleasure is exactly the same as pain in this regard. It has a beginning and an end, and it passes through the physical body and the nervous

Lesson Six

system and the brain, and that's it. I learned that joy was becoming free of all illusions of separation.

Imagine that the depth of your mind was truly like a spacious ocean that could contain all waves that arise within the field of the body-mind without any resistance at all, without being disturbed in its depth. There could be a great storm on the surface, but the depth of the ocean is undisturbed. Joy is a quality of awareness that is brought about through the release of illusions and the correction of how the mind thinks and how the heart feels. Joy is a quality of being that is not dependent on health or disease, money or poverty, birth, death, loss, or gain. To gain something in the world does not increase joy. It may, temporarily, give you pleasure.

That should give you enough to think about in regard to that part of your question.

Why have certain spiritual traditions denounced or sought to have their practitioners get out of the pleasure trap? Well, frankly, just because of this. Because the human mind *equates* pleasure with joy. And therefore, when unpleasurable sensations, such as sadness, such as confusion or doubt, or such as a physical sensation from an illness is passing through the body, the mind wants to get out of that state and create a different state. But that is merely the realm of duality in which there is no freedom.

True joy comes when no passing state of feeling in the body is denied or judged, but rather, embraced and experienced because that mind realizes it is not the passing state—it is not limited or identified with the passing state. The *joy-filled mind* can cry like no one has ever cried before. The joy-filled mind can embrace sadness to the depth, the greatest depth, that could be imagined. The joy-filled mind is the mind that observes all

The Way of Knowing

things, trusts all things, allows all things, embraces all things, transcends all things.

Joy, then, is a quality of *Knowingness*. Pleasure is a *physiological* state — very temporary — of the body-mind. Why, then, would any spiritual teacher say,

> *Be very careful. Don't seek pleasure.*

Simply because the mind can become addicted to confusing joy and pleasure. And therefore, whenever things aren't going right, it will try to recreate a temporary pleasurable state in the body. But all that does is continue the rut of the mind's misidentifying itself as the body. It keeps it in the realm of temporality and not in the realm of the eternal.

Now does that mean that you should refuse pleasure? Absolutely not! Just don't seek it. What do I mean by that? I have said to you many times that the body cannot be used to *get*. It can only be used to *give*. The Healed Mind does not need to use the body to get anything, for It sees that the body is merely a temporary communication device. It receives communications from other forms of life, other beings — rocks, trees, and human beings, and the wind and the waves and the stars — and It communicates Itself, It communicates Mind, through the body.

Many, for instance, in the realm of sexuality, are trying to *use* the body to *get* something called the pleasurable state because they think that pleasure is the same as joy. But the Awakened Mind, no longer misidentifying joy and pleasure, allows pleasurable states to pass through the body-mind, but only as a secondary effect of Its decision to use the body to enjoin with sexuality for the sole purpose of communicating to another:

Lesson Six

I see you in your perfect innocence and would celebrate it by joining with you whole-bodily.

So It is involved in *giving*, and the pleasurable states, that may or may not come and are always perhaps a little different, are only secondary. And that afterward, that Mind doesn't give it a second thought. It doesn't say,

Wow. The lights and bells and whistles didn't come on. It just wasn't what it should have been.

That kind of mind is involved in *getting*, because it needs pleasure, because it believes that pleasure is the same as joy.

Joy is the recognition that,

I and my Father are One. And in all contexts, I can choose Love over fear.

Therefore, indeed, there is a reason that many spiritual traditions have warned its students about the pleasure thing. Often that has gotten misinterpreted and gone beyond the point of its usefulness. If a mind *denies* or *suppresses* pleasure, it has the same effect as the mind that becomes *addicted* to pleasurable states. It will put out as much energy to *resist* a passing physiological state as the addicted mind will put into *seeking* pleasurable states. Either one is imprisonment.

Therefore, my suggestion for you is: Do not seek pleasure, but rather, seek the Kingdom. Be the presence of Love. And when pleasurable sensations pass through your awareness in the body-mind, notice them, accept them, and be done with them. Just like when so-called unpleasurable states—sadness, anger, fear, whatever it is that is arising—notice it, embrace it, let it pass through. Get on with being the presence of Love.

Does that help you in regard to your question?

Response: Yes.

Jeshua: Did it bring any illumination?

Response: [laughing] Yes.

Jeshua: Then indeed, beloved friend, remember: The body simply cannot accomplish *getting* anything. It *can* be used for grand things — the extension of Love. That, in itself, usually will generate acceptable, passing, pleasurable sensations.

Do you have anything else, then?

Question: Yes. The Shanti Christo board had a phone conference today, and I asked if anybody had any questions for this tape. And they suggested that we just ask you if you could speak to us — the board and the members as well — about the direction we're going and anything that you would care to address about the frequency of Shanti Christo and what we can do to keep our frequencies in alignment with the vision.

Answer: First, the frequency of Shanti Christo is unchanged, unchanging, and unchangeable forever. Simply because it *is* the *Peace of Christ*. But remember that peace is not a passive state at all. Rather, it is the foundation, the very empowering foundation, from which one accepts the pebble in the pond of the Will of God and knows that it is unlimited forever — with all power necessary to do *whatever* is asked. Such a mind is very powerful. Such a mind might be *extremely active* in the world. Such a mind remains at peace.

What can you do, then, *for* the vibration of Shanti Christo? Absolutely nothing. What you can do for *yourself* is want more of it. In that way is the vibration or frequency of Shanti Christo extended into the world. I once said that Love merely attracts the seeker of Reality to Itself.

God, then, pours Himself out into the world by becoming so attractive that His creations—the minds that populate the world—want more of Him. And they open to receive what is present.

Therefore, if you would serve the extension of Shanti Christo, be ever-vigilant to discipline the mind to want *only* more of God—for yourself. As you open to more of God, and *wait on no one*, other minds will decide whether or not they are willing to release what is obstructing them from receiving more of God. And then you'll be guided in how to create a context that might allow that to occur. Not that the context *causes* it. It merely gives the other mind permission to do so.

Do not become overly attached to the form or the accomplishment, but rather to the frequency you are allowing yourself to live within. Remember that all things are perfect. You need not be concerned about—hmm, shall we say—being a model, being a way-shower. You should not be concerned, whatsoever, with satisfying everybody who's looking for God who might come your way.

Rather, see that *you* are releasing the impurities that block the pure presence of God's Love: specialness, egotism, denial, fear, what you would call as I've heard you term it "Going up and out instead of down and in"—thinking instead of feeling. "Thinking instead of dancing," would be my way of saying it. Are you extending Love? Are you giving freedom to each and every mind, wanting only that mind to experience greater joy, letting them have their freedom in how they discover that. Are you awaking each morning with appreciation and joy, knowing that Shanti Christo has already been fulfilled and manifested? Are you delighting in allowing it to manifest in such a way that *you* learn something new about the nature of mind, the power of consciousness, and the Reality of Love?

If indeed, then, you would serve the vibration of Shanti Christo, you must be a *creator* and not a *maker*. But remind all of this: making is not the same as taking action. A mind can be involved in making by *refraining* from taking action. Does that make sense for you? Therefore, trust all things, allow all things, celebrate all things, see the perfection of all things, and *be* the vibration of Shanti Christo.

That should be enough for now.

Do you have anything else?

Response: No.

Jeshua: Very well. Therefore, we'll bring this question and answer session to an end.

And yet, I would say unto all of you—each and every one of you who will hear these words now, and even fifty years from now—remember always that the One who speaks to you through the vibration of these vocal cords is indeed that One who walked upon your plane as a man some two thousand years ago and delights only in extending Creation. Who looks upon you as a brother and as a friend, and who sees only your perfect innocence and delights in communicating with the only begotten Child of God—you!

Be you, therefore, at peace. And *Know* you are loved.

Amen.

Lesson Six

PERSONAL NOTES

The Way of Knowing

PERSONAL NOTES

Lesson Seven

Lesson Seven

Now, we begin.

And indeed, once again, greetings unto you, beloved and holy friends. As always, and though I have repeated this to you often, I say it to you again, and yet again: It is with *joy* that I come forth to abide with you, for *relationship is* the holiest of all places . . . relationship between any two who choose to look upon each other, having looked within and found no lack. For those two can then look out upon one another and see only perfect innocence, only perfect peace, only perfect Love.

Therefore, it *is* with joy that I join with you, for I look upon you with perfect peace, and perfect Love, and *perfect trust*. My *loyalty* to you is unshakable. No event that occurs in the realm of your space and time can *taint* the *loyalty* which I know to the depth of Truth that is your very Self: that which is unshakable, unchanging, unchangeable, and unchanged, forever. For my loyalty is perfectly pure. My trust of you is unfathomable and immeasurable.

How can this be so? For perhaps, even now, your mind says:

> *Well, yes, but last week I got a little angry with my spouse, and three weeks ago I forgot to pay for that candy bar I picked up in the store. Since I'm such a horrible dirt bag, your loyalty, Jeshua, is misplaced.*

My trust in you emerges *from* my trust in my Father. My trust in you emerges from the perfect knowledge that you belong *only* to That One that I have called *Abba*. My trust, then, is the expression of what I have come to know as I have looked in the depth of my own being, both within my physical incarnation that became rather famous, and also since then, where I discovered the perfection of Love that pervades all things, and can be seen beneath the surfaces, through the appearances that the body's eyes and the ego's thought system would show to you.

What do I mean by that? As you abide in your physical world, the greatest challenge that you have, moment to moment, and moment to moment, is to be vigilant against identifying with the perceptions which are born and birthed as a result of the physical apparatus of the body, itself. That is, you look out through a body; that is where your attention seems to be. And your apparatus, called your eyes, immediately shows you a world of objects separated by space. If you identify with that level of perception, you can only conclude that you are separate, one from another. And when you see events happening, it is absolutely impossible to see the subtle interconnection of all events. You fall into the trap of forgetting that you live in the Universe. And *universe* means, simply, "one turning," or "one song" — one event occurring, like an ocean is but one event, expressing as many waves. So, too, do all events in the field of space and time, in the field of physical matter, merely emerge from that *one* Universe.

From the body's level of perception, the thinking mind, in association with the body, creates *interpretations* of what it *believes* it is seeing. And now, your attention, your awareness, is already twice removed from reality. First, you have become hoodwinked, thinking that what the body's eyes show you is what is truly real and significant. For instance, you love someone. They are here today and tomorrow they leave. You see them pack their things and their body leaves, and your *eyes* show you that they are "gone."Then the mind says,

Woe is me. I have lost my love.

Neither of these is true.

Lesson Seven

The soul, the level at which Reality is far deeper than the level of the body, can never "go" anywhere. No one you've ever met or known can ever be outside of your heart through their *own action*. The body-mind, yes, can leave, but that is not what takes someone out of your *heart*. It can only be *your* decision to *withdraw love*. It is only the withdrawing of love that creates separation in the experience of your awareness.

So there you're sitting, two levels removed from Reality. First, you have become hoodwinked, thinking that the physical eyes show you what is true. Then you draw conclusions and create *interpretations* of the events the body's eyes show you. This creates the *emotional effect* that is like a soup that runs through you and around you, and will remain so—until it is healed.

The third level of being removed from Reality is the trick of the mind in which it *insists* that its interpretations are fact. It is to this level of the mind that I asked within A *Course in Miracles*,

> *Would you rather be* right *or* happy?

For happiness can be only the result of perfect *trust*. And perfect trust emerges from a perfect *loyalty*. And a perfect loyalty emerges spontaneously in the mind that has rested in *surrender*.

We've spoken often of the Keys to the Kingdom: desire, intention, allowance, surrender. In allowance, you go through a period of deep undoing, in which you, in a sense, disconnect the wiring that has led you to *insist* on the rightness of the interpretations that *you* have created and then linked to events that the physical body-mind has perceived. So, as allowance is perfected, one has come to see that their whole world, everything they've constructed, has been *undone*. That is, your perception of belief, your perception of feeling nature, your perception of what is, has been undone. The mind is unraveled.

Now, the perception of the body-mind, of course, goes on. The physical eyes seem to show you that there is someone in another body over there, and they're doing what they're doing, and you're doing what you're doing, so there can't be any connection. That level goes on as long as there's a body. However, the mind that is healing does not *identify* that as the *primary level* of Reality.

And so, as allowance surrenders the construct that has been made up in the mind and exists nowhere but in the mind — one rests in an unobstructed allowance of how the body-mind goes through its days until it returns to dust. But there is no longer a "being hoodwinked," no longer being attached, no longer being swept up with that level of identification, because there is no longer a need to identify with the interpretations. And there is no longer — quite happily — any need to be right.

As allowance comes to completion, something quite magical occurs. It is beyond all comprehension of the thinking mind. The ego could never comprehend this! It is as though something which was existing because it was contracted in fear dies and dissolves, like the mist before a rising sun. And all that is left is a *quiet spaciousness* in which awareness has been purified. Events still arise and pass away. One continues to talk with their friends, perhaps as they always have. One notices the tendency in the body-mind to create interpretations; and some of them are quite necessary,

> *That light just turned red. My interpretation is that it might be wise to stop.*

But there is now something that is wrapped around all of that, so that what is arising is seen as, ultimately, quite inconsequential, quite innocent and devoid of any deep value. For you will place your *loyalty* on what you have *decided* to value. And in that spaciousness, in that perfect stillness, in that deep peace, mind — or *self*hood — dissolves in surrender.

Anyone who has awakened knows exactly what that feels like. Anyone who has begun to awaken has touched on moments of perfect surrender. For in surrender, the mind beholds that all things that are arising and passing away are perfectly harmless. They can hold no value, because they abide in time. And the things of time are like the waves that arise from the ocean — because they have a beginning, they *will* have an end. And in their beginning, their end is certain. And only a fool would create *loyalty* to that which is temporary, temporal and ultimately, unfulfilling. But the wise of heart have decided to place their value on that which is eternal. And what can be eternal, save God? And God *is* but Love.

Therefore, in *The Way of the Heart*, and in *The Way of Transformation*, and now, in *The Way of Knowing*, all that we have sought to share with you has been by design, to lead you to see that *Love* is the only thing worth valuing.

Love is unconditional. Love merely loves in order to abide in Its own nature. And because God is but Love, as the mind disentangles itself from the perceptual level of the body-mind, from the interpretations selected and created in the mind and overlaid over those events, and especially as it disentangles itself from the egoic need to be right about its *makings*, that which you are — pure intelligence, pure infinite creative possibility — shifts itself into being identified only with valuing Love. This is the same thing as saying,

I value only God.

Then, the soul begins to reawaken — this drop of pure Light, which is pure intelligence — the soul begins to realize that know God it must *be* God. And since God is only Love, the soul desires to be only Love. For in loving as God loves, God is known. And as God is known, Self is realized and remembered. And the dream of the dreamer is transcended.

Therefore, indeed, beloved friends, my *trust* in you is perfect, for I have come to value only God. My *loyalty* to *you* as the offspring of my Father stems from having received that enlightenment for myself, having awakened from the maze — the complex maze of perceptions in the body-mind, the interpretations that the body-mind places on events, and the ego's construct of what it feels it is right about. Because I have dissolved all of that, I abide in pure devotion only to what is *truly real* and *perfectly unconditional*: the presence of my Father, which is the same as the presence of Love.

Indeed, then, loyalty and trust . . . Look well to see what you have chosen to be loyal *to*. And if it is loyal to something of the world, you have actually been using loyalty as a way to overcome fear. Think about it. I have often said that what is not Love is only fear. In a state of Love, there is no clinging, there is no denial. There's nothing obstructed in the nature of the body's experience. One renders unto Caesar that which is Caesar's. One sweats in the hot summer sun. One simply is where one is, but the mind — the essence of your identity — is as Love. All of the rest of it is superfluous.

And so, you find yourself in a maze of events called space and time. By this, I mean you find yourself going to a job. You find yourself in a certain third-dimensional relationship. But you're not hoodwinked into thinking that this place, this context, is the all. It is only an opportunity for *you* to be the one who loves in the midst of that context, simply for the sake of knowing Love. And though the career, or the mate, or the car, or the flower, or the garden, or the boat — whatever it is that is begun in time ends in time—it can come and go. But your *delight* is in loving and embracing and being the field in which these events rise and fall.

If you are loyal to a person, place, or thing, look well to see: Is there, underneath, a fear that you have not yet been honest about? Are you being loyal in order to have this person, place, or thing approve of you and stay with you so that you get something that you want? And there's nothing wrong with that. Do not think that because you look and see,

> *You know, the bottom line is, I really like this job and the hundred and twenty thousand dollars a year that it pays me. I really like the sense of security that gives me.*

It doesn't mean you have to give it up and go live penniless on the street. What matters is that you become perfectly *honest* with what you're doing, and withdraw the tendency of the mind to say:

> *Well, I'm really doing this career because I really believe that the product that we create is making a huge impact on the planet. I believe we can really make things different. And besides, you know, we give jobs, and we give money to charities. And that's why I'm here.*

Oh, nonsense! In the world, you will do what you do because of where you place your value. This is why I've often said,

> *If you want to know truly what you idolize, what you are committed to, what you most deeply believe, merely look at where you are, who you're with, and what you're doing with your time, and how you feel about it — truthfully.*

Those that insist on saving up money for a rainy day are merely stating,

> *I believe there can be a rainy day, unless I do something to prevent it.*

Their trust has been placed in their power to manipulate and use the world to create what they perceive they must have. And it is very, very different than the trust of the one awakened in God who knows that whatever arises and passes away in the field of space and time is inconsequential. Because *that* mind is so identified with being the presence of Love that the body-mind could contract cancer tomorrow and,

> *Who cares!*

The mind that rests in freedom has learned to translate — to transfer — trust and loyalty to Love. That mind has come to enjoy the peace that comes with only loving. For what harm can come to the mind that simply loves . . . who looks upon all things and sees its perfect innocence and plays in the kingdom provided by that one's Father — the kingdom of the body-mind, the kingdom of space and time, the kingdom of the power to choose Love over fear?

This is why I suggested to this, my beloved brother, the simple thought: Suffering comes from being identified with *form*, whether it be the body, a belief, a career, a context of experience of any kind. For all experience comes and goes. Liberation and deep peace come from being identified with *content*. And by *content*, here, we simply mean *the matrix or the source* out of which all possibilities are, indeed, possible. It is like a musician who comes to appreciate the field of silence out of which notes can arise in a certain temporal order, in order to create a beautiful melody. If it were not for the silence between the notes, no song could have ever touched your heart.

The matrix of Love, which is the presence of the Father, the Pure Intelligence, the Field in which all things arise and pass away and never changes . . . that Field is like a canvas upon which the Grand Artist paints. But the master artist knows that without the canvas, there is nothing, and, therefore, *honors* the blank canvas *first*.

Loyalty and trust are significant things to ponder. Each time — and there is a process of growth, of course — each time you begin to see that what you have placed your trust in cannot really, truly, fulfill the soul, it is as though a structure crumbles. Now, what is actually occurring? You, as infinite being, have merely realized that you have been hoodwinked, that's all. And you are withdrawing value from what you placed your trust in. That feels like a crumbling. And it literally is a crumbling at the subtle level of energy that constructs a perceptual belief system about the nature of experience.

For instance, to give you a simple example, if one believes that they must have coffee every morning in order to get going, and then later in life, for whatever reason, they come to see that they never needed it at all, they may go ahead and enjoy their coffee, but it will never be for the same reason. That structure of belief will crumble and they will literally see life differently.

And each and every one of you can pause this tape right now and merely ponder what structures of belief have crumbled in your life. Has it not always led to a sense of greater expansion, deeper wisdom, a more certain Knowing?

In other words, life proceeds from illusion to Reality. And as the soul awakens, it, literally, feels a sense of expansion and growth. But the growth has nothing at all to do with the body getting bigger, or the bank account growing, or having more children. You all know that as wisdom is reawakened in the mind, there is a sense of growth. And that kind of growth becomes all-attractive to you.

When you become so much a *lover* of the wisdom of perfect union with God, so that that's all that matters to you, you're already ninety percent free of illusion. And the world will never have the power to truly bind you again. Place, then, your trust in the Love that birthed you. And when I say, "birthed you," I am NOT talking about the body. I am NOT talking about your personal history, your ego. The "you" that I refer to exists within and prior to all of that. It is as though your Father has created you as the powerful ocean in which *you* have been— knowingly or unknowingly—emanating all of the waves that have become your particular experience as the soul. *That* is what God has created. Trust the One that created *you* as an *infinite source of awareness* that is perfectly free in every moment to decide what experience it will have.

Why is this important? You see, your world would teach you, and the level of perception of the body-mind would say,

> *Well, I want to have an experience. Oh, I just had a thought of having an ice cream cone. Well, I've experienced driving my body to the ice cream store and eating ice cream.*

That event does occur. But if you look closely, you'll discover that your *experience* is the *value you* place *upon the* event. I know that seems subtle to you, but it's very, very important. *Experience actually occurs nowhere but in the field of the mind.*

Lesson Seven

You could just as easily go to store and eat ice cream and have your mind on a book that you're writing, or the remembrance of a great love affair or a great movie from the night before, and never even notice the taste of the ice cream. And you get home, and your wife or husband says,

> *Well, dear, did you have a good trip to the ice cream store?*
>
> *Oh! Oh, that's right. I think I did stop ... I ...You know, to tell you the truth, I don't even remember what I had!*

So where does experience occur? It does *not* occur at the level of the body-mind itself. It occurs at the level of *mind*. And *mind shapes experience according to what it chooses to value.*

Now, does that mean that you just drop doing anything in the world? No. An Awakened being in the world simply delights and has fun — *from a state of clarity of knowing* that whatever they choose to do with the body-mind is merely a free choice based on what they're choosing to value in the moment. And if they own that valuation, they can totally enjoy the experience they're having.

And then, they have come full circle. If they want to design a website, if they want to be a banker, if they want to be a dancer, a prostitute, a farmer — *it no longer matters*! For the mind that is awake, while the body lasts, merely sees experience arise and pass away.

It takes total ownership and realizes that *It* has the power to create its experience as being delightful, fulfilling, and a blessing — *regardless* of what the body-mind is actually doing.

The Way of Knowing

There can be no difference, you see. It doesn't matter if you are a teacher standing at the shores of a great lake in what you now call your Israel, standing at a boat, talking to a hoard of hundreds, or perhaps seeing if you can actually make a few fish and loaves of bread feed five thousand,

Oh! How about that! That was fun!

There is no difference between that and driving a truck in New York City and delivering frozen fish, if the mind within the soul is taking complete ownership and delighting in the mystery of creating experience, and chooses to bring enjoyment and freedom to that moment.

This is why events of the world can never bind you. All suffering comes because of the interpretation you are *overlaying* over events. And in that very moment, you have used God's gift to you, which is the *power* of awareness, to create its experience.

Once again, my crucifixion was my final learning lesson in the realization that I had broken the spell. I was no longer under the spell of the egoic mind, or the body-mind. I merely looked upon my experience and decided to freely be in a state of Love in the midst of that context.

You are free to be in a state of Love in the midst of any context, as you watch and observe the waves of temporality come and go. And as you see that happen, and as you develop that capacity within yourself — through the *choices* for Love, through the *choices* for forgiveness, through the *choices* to be happy instead of right, to live in innocence and wonder instead of certainty and dread, to rest in True Knowledge, True Knowing, rather than the relative knowledge of the world — you come to see that all that is arising and passing away can never leave you, that loss is impossible. For where the mind chooses to rest in

Lesson Seven

Love, all things that arise and pass away are remembered and restored and sanctified. There is perfect peace.

And though a beloved friend passes away in what you call "death," because you do not identify the friend with the body-mind, because you do not, then, perceive that you can no longer love your friend, you just enjoy loving your friend. And as you abide in *Love*, you begin to experience the Reality that nothing dies. Nothing dies! For pure intelligence can go nowhere. You had one of your scientists once say:

> *Well, how about this! I think I have figured it out. Energy is what makes up everything, and it can never go anywhere. It can only change form. But the essence, or the energy, remains.*

This is not unlike a mystic, or a sage, or a great savior or messiah, or a very ordinary everyday person waking up and going:

> *You know, only Love is Real! And in Love, all things exist forever. I'm not separate. I am not lost. I am free!*

The great journey in the field of space and time is to allow that awareness to settle into your beingness so that that quality of awareness *permeates* and *pervades* the level of the egoic mind, the level of interpretation, and the level of perception, or energy, at the level of the body-mind—the apparatus of the nervous system brain. All of that's still going on, but you begin to *pervade* it with the growing awareness that only Love is Real, that,

I have the power to extend forgiveness.

Every time the mind trusts in the One that created it, and rests in that peace, a miracle occurs. Every time that you have extended forgiveness, a miracle has occurred, for you have withdrawn valuation of an old perceptual system and chosen for Reality. The enlightened sage is merely one who has cultivated the practice of training the mind to choose for the Reality of Love under all circumstances. And through that one's many successes, they have come to know that what they have chosen is true. God has been revealed. *Loyalty* is no longer a question.

Trust and loyalty, then, must flow from the mind in its power to choose what it will value. Be you, therefore, *loyal* to Love. Be you, therefore, *loyal* to your perfect union with God. *Trust* That One who birthed you and who has been guiding your journey home all along. For remember, I have said often, that from the very moment the dream of separation began to be dreamed, already the answer was provided, called the Holy Spirit, the right-mindedness in the depth of your being that cannot be touched.

Rest in the right-mindedness of choosing only Love. Extend complete freedom to the *waves* that come and go. And in this sense, the weather is a wave, Caesar is a wave, your spouse is a wave; that is, as you would look at them as a body-mind. They are a wave. They will come and they will go. But if you abide in the Field of Love, you abide in timelessness and eternity. You abide as the spaciousness that embraces all things, trusts all things, and thereby, transcends all things.

Here, then, beloved friends, is the pure essence of loyalty and trust: If your *loyalty* is in anything that can crumble, you have merely not yet fully chosen to place your loyalty in that which cannot crumble. If your *trust* is in a requirement that individuals act and behave in a certain way, you have not yet come to trust the perfection of Love that is already at work in everyone's lives, calling them to deeper levels of remembrance.

See, then, the perfection of all events. For the waves that arise in the temporality called the world have no power, in and of themselves. They are already held in the arms of a perfectly loving God, and each event *truly* serves no purpose save to nudge that soul, that spark of pure awareness or intelligence, to look deeper beyond its illusions.

When anyone attacks you or projects upon you, they are merely crying out in their own fear and insanity. The Awakened One looks upon them with Love and merely says,

> *Oh, is that so? Well, very well. Yes, thank you for sharing. Have a nice day,*

and goes on trusting and lets their life be an expression of the loyalty that they give *only* to the Voice of the Holy One within them.

Trust and loyalty. Another way to approach the subject is to simply look and see,

> *Where are my idols? What am I attached to, and why?*

Remember that those with thoughts of "I" and "mine" know not the true nature of things. When you say, "my car," or "my wife," you're not dealing with Reality, for all things belong to God. There is nothing that you can possess *except* the Reality of what you *are* as the Thought of Love in form.

Come to see, then, that when you choose Love, you become free. Who can harm you? What gain or loss can affect your peace? And in each moment, as you remember Love, you give Love. And everywhere you go, and everyone you see, is touched in a quiet and secret place. They may not know why they feel attracted to being in your presence, but *you* will know. You are simply choosing to *be*—and mark my words well here—you are merely choosing to finally *awaken* and *be* GOD INCARNATE. For God is but Love, and when you love, there is only God.

Remember then always, beloved friends, that that which crumbles can only be form and not content. Love can never crumble, because it is the content which is the presence of God's Reality. Because Love is content, it is unchangeable, unchanged, and unchanging forever. Perfect freedom comes to any mind that *shifts its identity* from the level of the body, from the level of the interpretive mind, from the level of the egoic mind that *insists* its constructs are real and correct and valuable, and becomes identified with Love.

Identity with what is conditional and temporal can never produce what is *unconditional and atemporal, or eternal. The power of mind can leap from the conditioned to the unconditional, through the decision to place value only on that.*

Well do I understand that what arises within the body-mind is a fear of survival. And yet, it is a useless fear, since the body-mind, from the moment of its conception, has been marching inexorably toward its demise. And if the body-mind, itself, is completely *powerless* (which it is) to exist as eternity, everything dependent on the body-mind must crumble with it. Everything,

Lesson Seven

then, built as a house upon the foundation of your having become identified with the perceptual level of the body-mind, the interpretations of the thinking mind, and the insistence of the egoic mind on being right — these are all like floors in a house built on a foundation of error and illusion — you might as well own it now: they are going to crumble.

Illusions have no life. That is what makes them illusions. Only in Reality is Life finally found. Yes, you do feel that crumbling going on, for what crumbles in the mind sends a shock wave, like a ripple, down through the body-mind, through the brain, through the nervous system, and the body shakes and groans, and maybe it complains and cries, but it's nothing more than the crumbling of illusion.

Eventually, the body, itself, must crumble as an illusion. For the mind that grows in the radiance of its awakening must finally put away the entire physical dimension as a toy outgrown. The body-mind, the nervous system, can no longer contain you, for what you *value is* the radiance of merely *being the* presence of God's Love. You begin to realize that you don't need a body-mind at all to operate, in order to extend Love. *While* the body-mind *lasts*, love it, embrace it, allow it, don't expect great things from it, just use it as a temporary communication device.

Since what you want is Love, practice teaching *only* Love. Teaching Love is not talking *about* Love, not about the philosophy of Love, not about the metaphysics of Love. You teach Love by *being loving* in each moment. And you can only be loving by allowing yourself to *feel* the presence of Love *in* and *as* your moment-to-moment experience.

Because Love is unconditional, you are free now. No set of circumstances must change *before* you have the power to be in Love. This is the same things as saying that God is given to you by Grace in each moment, and you are asked only to open and receive. Only Love is Real. Only Love allows you to transcend the great fear, the great suffering, that comes only from a temporary, mistaken identity problem—an authority problem. You think your construct of the world is your authority. You think the body-mind is who you really are. This is merely an identity problem, an authority problem. When you come to know that you are merely the expression of That One—Pure Spirit, Love—you are free from the world.

Now, will the world "get it?" Will the world go,

Oh, well gee! I'm really glad that you are free. Gee whiz!

Of course not, since the world is the attempt to be *other* than the Truth of the Kingdom. Therefore, when anyone projects upon you at any time, when anyone is in any way anything *but* loving, it can only be because they are still choosing to insist on the rightness of their construct of the sensory data, that has come through their nervous system, which they have been identified with. In other words, they're living in illusions.

Only Love is Real. And if you want to be with one who is sane and awake, be only with one who chooses to teach only Love. Let *those* be your friends. Let *those* be your playmates. Let *those* be your lovers and your spouses, for only they are capable of honoring the Truth that is true always, and seeing it as the very essence of your soul. That is why there is a great attraction to anyone who is awake, for they "see" you. They see you to your *essence*, because they see *from* their own. These two are but one and the same, for the Holy Son of God is One. Choose, therefore, Love and transcend the suffering that is the world.

Look well, then, beloved friends, over the next thirty days. Enjoy merely looking at where you have placed your loyalty in

Lesson Seven

the past, where you are placing it now. And look at the grand journey that you've made. What on earth has changed your loyalty from your teddy bear to God, if not God, Herself?

Think not, then, that you have been apart from that One. For in each moment of your experience, even as you believed in the illusions that the body's eyes would show you, already That One, who is but Love, was working to dissolve your illusions, one by one, in the way unique to the dynamics of your own soul.

When the ship sails into the harbor, it is Home. The long journey is forgotten. And, perhaps, there will be a few stories told in the pub as everyone has a beer. But in a day or two, a week or a month, the journey fades from awareness. And friends merely abide together, growing flowers, dancing in the evenings, observing the sunset, giving hugs and kisses. When the ship sails into the harbor, the journey is over. And there is only calm water, though around it the storm may rage. Let it! *Let the storm of life rage*. Merely identify with the peace beyond all understanding, the peace that comes as a mind comes to choose only identity with Love. Peace, beloved friends, is the result of the *shift of identity* which emerges by placing your trust and loyalty only in That One who is only Love.

Allow, then, everything else to crumble. And does that mean you must give up your golden coins? Of course not! For that would be to say that the golden coins have a power to bind you. They do not! Neither the having of them or the lack thereof can bind you. Only your decision not to love can bind you and make you suffer.

Give, then, perfect freedom to all created things, for they belong not to you, nor were they given to you to give you security or to boost your ego, or to make you happy. They are given for your enjoyment and for you to bless, for the Christ who walks this Earth knows that His or Her primary purpose is to bless the Father's creations, to set all things free in the sanctity of their own deep and perfect union with God.

Seek to possess nothing or no one. Seek to change nothing and no one. Seek only to love. And in Love, you are set free.

So then, as we would end this time together, as you stop your tape, simply make the decision to spend five minutes doing nothing but loving all that you see through the body's eyes, all that you notice arising in the mind as a memory or an image of a friend, or what-have-you, or an event—any event that has occurred. Simply decide to love it, that's all. And then, try to tell yourself that peace is a long way off. It is present in every decision for Love.

Therefore, indeed, with perfect trust and perfect loyalty, I look upon you and already know that you are borne on the wings of that Love that carries you away to Itself. In perfect trust and loyalty I look upon the holy and only begotten Child of God, and *know* that the dream of separation has already been corrected, and you abide in perfect safety—now!

For the events of space and time can *never* touch or alter the Spirit, the Pure Intelligence, the Infinite Awareness, that *is* the Truth of who you are. It is up to you to decide to enjoy that Power of Awareness by selecting *only* loving thoughts.

Peace, beloved friends, be with you always.

Amen.

Lesson Seven

PERSONAL NOTES

The Way of Knowing

PERSONAL NOTES

Lesson Eight

Lesson Eight

Now, we begin.

And, indeed, once again, greetings unto you, beloved and holy friends. We would come forth to abide with you this day to speak, yet again, of the simple subject—to speak, yet again, of the essence of *all that you seek*. To speak, yet again, of the essence of *all that you are*. To speak, yet again, with great devotion, with unceasing praise, as we share with you—as we share one to another—that which alone can set God's Child free. That which *alone* enlightens the mind, purifies the heart, and brings about the serenity of the soul . . . *the serenity of the soul*.

What, then, could such a subject be? What *theme* could all of these words point to? Indeed, beloved friends, what does the morning sunrise point to? What does the sound of a child's laughter point to? Indeed, beloved friends, what does the very breath you breathe point to? What do all things of Creation point to? For I have said unto you before that there is nothing you can create that does not express your longing to awaken. Therefore, all "doing" of the body-mind is but the attempt of the soul to break free of all limitation and to, once again, rest, recline, in that perfect peace which is the *certain knowledge* that: *Only Love is Real*.

The yogi in his cave but expresses the longing of that one's soul to recline in God. The lovers, entwined, express only the longing of the soul to taste, to touch the Reality of Love. And Love is but God, for God *is* but Love. All things, then, reflect to you, through the sensory apparatus of the body-mind, the longing of all Creation to *know*, with perfect certainty, the living presence of That One whom I have called *Abba*.

Love, then—*LOVE*—is the subject of this month's sharing. For in *The Way of Knowing*, it must come to pass that the mind is converted from fear to Love, from doubt to *perfect faith*. And perfect faith is not that beginning and intermediate stage, in which one is *choosing* to have faith in things unseen in the hope that they might materialize, for perfect faith casts out all fear. Faith, then, when purified, when matured, when totally realized, is the same as complete forgiveness, the return to peace, and the K*nowledge* that only Love is Real.

Love, beloved friends, is the essence of all that you are. Love is the essence of *all* that dances as a temporary reflection before the eyes of your very body-mind. There is nothing you can look upon whose essence is *not* Love. There is *nothing* you can experience whose essence is not Love. The only question, then, is: Are you willing to make the journey from fear to Love, as you look upon anything, as you experience any emotion? For there can be nothing that obstructs from you the Light and Presence of your Creator. And to perceive the Real World of Love is to know, with perfect certainty, that you and your Father are One.

When you remember only your loving thoughts, Love is all that you will see. To "remember only your loving thoughts" does not just mean that as you look upon what you have been taught to call the "past" . . . yet, rest assured, if you're having a memory *now*, you're having a very *present* experience. It's absolutely *impossible* to think about the past, for thinking occurs *now*. And you will look upon the past as you *choose to be* in the present, choose to be as the presence of Love. And there is *not one event* that you have ever experienced as a soul, that is not immediately translated into perfect harmlessness, into the perfect realization that only a dream has occurred. For Love looks upon all things and sees that there is no substance to them, *except* the Love out of which those involved in that situation were *longing* to find a way to know the Reality of themselves.

Lesson Eight

Listen carefully here: There is nothing you can experience that is *anything but* the soul's *longing* to be the perfection of what it is: Love.

Your tall skyscrapers, your busy freeways, your armies — *everything* is an expression of the *longing of the soul*, that spark of divinity that rests in all created things, *to know Love*.

Has it become distorted? Oh, yes! To think that one can awaken to Love, to know Love, to have Love, by building weapons of destruction must be wholly insane. But the *longing* from which it arises is absolutely no different than the pacifist who would place a flower in the barrel of a rifle. It is no different than the mother who picks up and suckles her newborn son. The *longing* is one and the same!

This is why I have said often to you that what is not Love is fear, and nothing else. Fear is merely the contraction that has occurred in the soul, itself, that has lost, temporarily, the sanity of knowing that it need not *seek* for Love, it need only *open* and *be* Love. For the attempt to *seek* Love only reveals that sanity is not ruling the domain and the dominion of your heart and soul and mind.

Any attempt to *get* is insane. Likewise, any attempt to *refrain* from *receiving or giving* is *also* insane. Getting and receiving are not the same. Giving to get is not true giving. Giving and receiving are one. For in each case, the heart must open, the defenses must be laid aside, and the soul becomes *wholly vulnerable*.

And yet, in the perfect paradox of the spiritual journey, when *vulnerability* is fully allowed, through mastery of the Keys to the Kingdom (Desire, Intention, Allowance, Surrender), when this indeed is accomplished, Love is known. For in perfect vulnerability, the soul remembers its perfect *invulnerability*. And the world can do nothing to that one who only loves.

Oh, indeed, beloved friends, the beauty of every flower, the song of every bird that sings—these things are given to *you*, the *Holy* Son of God. The sparkling waters, the vast expanse of the desert—these things are given to *you*. There is no creation that has within it the capacity that you, as a human being, possess. Not even your whales and dolphins can truly experience and *realize* the presence and the mystery of the Creator. They flow in perfect innocence *in* creativity, *in* the Creator's Love, but their capacity to *reflect* and to *know*, and to *embody consciously* That which Love is, is not the same.

And those that would perceive that seeking out a whale, or a dolphin, or a wolf, or a bear, or a crow, or what-have-you, are yet caught up in *projecting* onto another form of creation that which must be embraced in and for *oneself*—for the body is the temple of the Living Spirit, when it is seen through eyes that have awakened. *Where you are is* where Heaven is fully available. *That which you are is* the Love of God made manifest. And when you "remember only your Loving thoughts," that means that in the very *present moment*, you are *remembering*, you are bringing the facets of yourself back into the wholeness of the realization that *only Love is Real*.

Yes, my dog just died. Yes, my husband just left me.

These are just the external forms bouncing about in the field of change:

But the essence has not left me, for I am free to love. I am free to make the energetic transition from one set of circumstances into the present moment. I am free in each moment not to abide in fear, not to abide in that great fear that I can't possibly survive because

Lesson Eight

my teddy bear has been stolen.

And what are husbands, and mates, and careers, and cars, and money in the bank, if not the attempt of the *little child* within you to have and hold onto the "teddy bear" that you think can comfort you? Yet, the *Christ* within you can *Love!*

In each moment, then, that you seem to be confronted with the challenge that brings up within you your deepest fears of security, your deepest fears of managing the estate — the domain that you call your "life" — these things come not by accident. And they *must* come *without ceasing* in a world of unceasing change. For all that you would look upon and say that you love, as you look upon it and perceive it as a temporary form of creation, it is already dying and dead to you. There can be no peace in the world. But you can be the *embodiment* of peace when you look beyond all form and perceive the *essence* of all things as the *longing for Love*, the *longing* to remember.

And when your spouse leaves you, no matter what they say, they are leaving you because they *long* for Love. Does this mean that you have failed them? *Absolutely not!* For that would mean that *they* are a victim of *you*. But you have heard me say unto you many times, there is no cause, save that which arises within the field of the sovereignty of each soul. Love is always present, and there is no reason for staying or going. There is only reason to awaken to the Voice for Love and to allow *It* to move *you*.

So in the world, peace cannot be found; for in the *world*, there is only the deep belief that Love is absent and must be sought, pursued, and *gotten* — extracted — from the forms of creation, whether it be career, flower, ocean, desert, lover, mate, money. The forms of the world contain no reality. By that, I mean that when you look at someone or something, and the energy of wanting to possess or extract runs you, you are already in insanity. Insanity is wholly *illusory*, which means any attempt to live from that energy can only fail.

And yet, in the very same moment, the world awaits you in *perfect transparency*. Nothing can obstruct you. In the busiest of your malls, in the most horrendous traffic jam, there is nothing that is preventing you from choosing to remember only your loving thoughts; to look upon a brother or a sister and to see their perfect innocence, to see their unchanging essence, while allowing them *complete freedom* to journey as they must, until they elect to remember that essence within themselves, until they have chosen to learn to be the stillness of God's presence.

Stillness is not opposed to activity or movement. Rather, it pervades the very body- mind. There is a stillness in the Awakened that is ever-attractive. And yet, the Awakened are ceaselessly involved. Why? Because they no longer resist the flow of this dream world, *including* the body-mind. They have reversed the thought structure of the world within themselves. The body-mind is no longer *compelled* by fear. Unobstructed, it serves but one purpose: the extension of Love. Can you extend Love by restraining the energy of the body? No. Can you extend Love by holding on to rigid thoughts and beliefs about how relationship should be? No.

The only way, then, to remember Love, the only way to rest in the certainty of *The Way of Knowing*, is to come to the realization that what is not Love is fear, and only fear. In any moment — any moment of experience — regardless of what is occurring, where Love is not present within you as a *known commodity*, you are in fear.

We do not speak here of the emotion, or the wave of energy, that might be passing through the body when you walk around the corner on a trail to behold a very angry mother — what you

Lesson Eight

call the — grizzly bear, who will, indeed, protect her cubs by having you for breakfast. Those are just emotions passing through the body-mind, part of the system that would help you to flee or to stay. Do not make the mistake of perceiving *that* as fear. It is just a biochemical, electrical impulse, programmed into the body-mind. For even the wise and enlightened will pay attention to that! And yet, the wise and enlightened will look quickly and see,

> *Perhaps this is my time – go ahead bear, eat me. Go ahead, crucify me.*

Hmm? Or perhaps, that very same enlightened one will say,

> *Take me from the city. The crowds are too great. We must flee across the lake, for they would press upon me and eat me up if they can. It is not time. This is not the place.*

Peace, then, is not a passivity. Peace, the very state of Love, is a state in which *no experience* is obstructed within you. Do not make the mistake, as so many do, of thinking that experience has something to do with what is outside of the very body-mind. For remember, *nothing* is *caused* by a single event occurring beyond the boundary of the body-mind.

If two human beings come together, they may not know why, but for some reason their heart is open, they're walking around with a neon sign that says,

> *I just want to love and be loved. That's the only Reality. I'm a little tired of putting up a wall of resistance.*

They walk around the corner — oh my goodness! The sparks fly.

> *Oh! Love! Love! This is it! It's like (what you call) the Coke – it's*

the real thing! This is it! Oh, my God! Oh! Oh! How could this be? Oh, this must be a gift from God.

Nonsense! It's a gift from yourself. *You* are the one who chose in the depth of your being to finally become *sane enough* to allow the context for the experience of Love's sharing to be called to you. And, guess what—it's occurring in your lover for the very same reason. It is just that two souls have sent out the call and have come together in a field of space-time, within the body-mind, for a moment, in which each has said "Yes" to the possibility of remembering the Purity of Love.

Love does not condemn, and Love does not judge. And what is not Love is fear, and nothing else. Therefore, remember always, precious friends, that *no* act of Love should ever be judged. For *each* act of Love is to be cherished. Each *moment* of Love's presence and Reality, each *moment* in which a soul, two souls, three souls, ten souls, a country of souls, a universe of souls—it doesn't matter—where the choice is made to drop the defenses, to *open* and *gesture* as the presence of Love—that act is to be *cherished!* For it is rare in the world.

Those that would seek to possess a mate, to create an *exclusivity*, are *truly* only expressing some subtle level of fear. For Love denies *not* to anyone the perfect freedom that is the sovereignty and right of every soul. For you cannot know Love until you have set all beings free. You cannot know your Creator until you love as your Creator loves. And there is no one who is listening to these words, there's no one who's ever chosen to listen to this attempt to communicate through a body-mind, through collaboration, through creative joining, that which reflects the wisdom of Reality, there's no one who has ever listened to these words, that does not long to know Love completely, to come Home again.

Lesson Eight

To "come Home" means to know Love. And to know Love means that you can no longer tell where you end and the Creator begins. Such a one merely loves. Such a one rests in the perfect certainty of Love so deeply that the thought of restricting another's freedom *cannot arise*. Why would it? If your cup is truly overflowing, would you require another to place their half-filled glass before you, demanding that you need to possess their glass? Love *allows* all things. Love *embraces* all things. Love *trusts* all things, and thereby, *immediately transcends* all things.

If you would, then, know Love, in this the year of *The Way of Knowing*, spend the next thirty days, in which in *each day, without fail* — remember it is wise to use time constructively — spend some time each day in which you abide with yourself and a piece of paper and a pencil, and truly look back over your past — honestly: Where did you refuse to give total freedom to the ever-changing expressions of Creation?

Have you ever judged a politician? In that very moment, you were refusing to extend perfect freedom, for judgment flows from fear and not from Love. Were you ever in a relationship in which some part of you felt at least a little urge to try to convince the other that they don't really love that person they met in the supermarket, they really love just you? Have you ever, even politely for a moment, insinuated to another that their passion for anyone but you might be some sort of "biological abnormality," or certainly, they're being insane and need to sit down and do some serious thinking?

All of that is fear, and nothing else. For Love is satiated in its own being. Love overflows. And the thought of possessing, controlling, or limiting can come only from one who feels emptiness. Love sets all things free. Love sets the world free to be as the world is. Love sees perfect harmlessness. Love sees that because things are as they are, they are as they are. Think well about that statement... Because things are as they are, the mind in perfect freedom lets them *be* as they are, and sees them as utterly harmless.

Love sees, then, that the world that is shown to you through the body-mind — this world of buildings, this world of automobiles and pollution and pristine beaches and desert expanses and towering trees and lakes and ponds, this world of torment in the mother whose child has just died, this world of torment in the heart of a child who has just buried their parent, this world of torment, this world of peace, this world that contains all possible expressions of consciousness — *this world is perfectly harmless*. This world that you experience *in this now moment* cannot add anything to you, and it can take nothing away.

This *now* moment, beloved friends, where are you? Are you *in Love*, in this moment? Did you just lose your job? And you think the problem that is disturbing your peace is that you have no job? That's not it. What's disturbing your peace is that the loss of job has flushed up for you your deep identity with, and as, the body. You think the body *must* survive and continue, and,

> *Darn it, it has to do it in the same level of material comfort that I knew yesterday!*

Can you understand that when your Love is so complete, it no longer matters if the body-mind exists tomorrow? For where would you go? You are but the Field of Love Itself. Your essence is unchanging forever. You are Pure Spirit.

If you just lost your job, sit down and breathe and open the heart and decide to love your employer unto the death of your illusion. Then, open and receive all that is around you — the

Lesson Eight

singing of the bird, the first rays of a new day's dawn, the grasses beneath your feet, the field of infinite possibilities that has been thrown *wide open for you*. For that which passes away in your experience cannot do so by accident. It can only be occurring through the complicity, or the agreement, of the world around you with the world, or the soul, within you. *Nothing arises by accident.*

And if you come home to discover that your child has died sleeping in her crib, feel indeed your feelings, with great curiosity.

> *Oh, this is how a human being feels when they perceive that loss has occurred. I will bring Love to this moment and feel this as deeply as I can, because I want to embrace it with Reality.*

Then look with gentleness upon that tiny form of lifelessness, and know that the *soul* who animated it for a brief moment has gone no where, except into the furtherance of their destiny *and yours*—always by *perfect agreement*. Not the kind of an agreement in which a child says,

> Yes, Mom. Yes, Dad. Whatever you say.

But the agreement of the perfect sovereignty of two unlimited souls.

You have heard me say before that the spiritual path cannot begin until a mind accepts *complete responsibility* for the entire field of its experience. This must include the comings and goings of all beings.

> *I called them in, I called to them and asked them to leave me. I wonder why I did that? Oh, God! Here's this feeling again. I'm all alone. I've been abandoned. That's why they've had to leave me*

The Way of Knowing

... For I must heal this ridiculous belief that I have been abandoned. I must overcome all separation. I must awaken beyond the dream of the dreamer.

Nothing you create can arise by accident. And nothing you experience but calls you to the field of unchanging and perfect Love that transcends, supersedes, and underlies all that arises and passes away.

Love, indeed, beloved friends. For we are coming down to the conclusion of this *Way of Knowing*. *The Way of Knowing* must be the *completion* of the *decision to teach only Love*. And the only way to teach Love is to *be Love under all circumstances*. This does not mean that you paint a plastic smile on your face and never feel any emotion. That is not enlightenment. *That* is the *height* of the ego's attempt to usurp power from God. For the spiritual ego, the spiritual personality, is indeed the last "egg" to be cracked. For only that one is awakened who *allows* all things, *trusts* all things, *embraces* all things—which is the same as to say, *feels* all things. For in that very moment, the very thing arising is transcended because it is not obstructed or resisted. And what is not obstructed or resisted is, indeed, embraced, *consumed* in the spaciousness of Love.

You have within yourself, then, all power under Heaven and Earth to translate the body itself from a contraction of fear to a spaciousness that reflects the Reality of God's Love. For the very body-mind that emerged first, from fear, can be *reopened*, so that the energy of Truth flows through it, so that nothing arising in your experience in the emotional field . . . And quite frankly, the emotional field is the *only* place you can experience anything—the rest of it is merely thoughts *about* things. And the gap between a thought *about* things and the feeling nature of *experiencing* things is exactly the same gap that exists between Heaven and illusion. It is for this reason that no *idea* of

Lesson Eight

God is the same as God. No *concept* about Love is the same as Love. No *philosophy* about enlightenment is the same as enlightenment.

Unobstructed feeling embrace of all that arises and passes away — *unobstructed* means without judgment. Even that which arises as fear or anger should never be judged or obstructed. That which arises as sadness or joy, that which arises as the passion of the body, all things must be *opened to* and *embraced* — or the beingness of your soul has not yet transcended the world.

Love, then, is the ability to be wholly present with what is, devouring it like a child devours candy:

Hmm! Give me another bite. For this dream cannot contain me. Therefore, bring it on!

And so, indeed, beloved friends, if you would truly use this year of *The Way of Knowing* as the year in which you awaken into the decision to be the presence of Love and *nothing else*, before this year ends — so that you can move into the rest of your experience *as* the Enlightened Christ that you already are — look well, then, in each of the next thirty days:

Where in my life have I refrained from Love?

Where have I chosen behavioral patterns and decisions and choices with a smile on my face, while all the time, attempting to control and manipulate the world in order to keep me safe from feeling and facing my own insecurities?

Where have I demanded that the world show up in a certain way so that I can pretend to have peace, where I can pretend to be happy and loving?

The Way of Knowing

For anyone can be happy and loving in a candy store. Anyone can be happy standing in front of a crowd, and everyone's applauding you. Anyone can be happy being held by twenty friends who say they love you. But only the enlightened can be happy when those twenty friends have chosen to crucify you. Therefore, indeed, it is in your *darkest* moments, it is in the *crumbling* of the structures you have made, where you are best given the opportunity to realize the great power within you to teach only Love.

And yet, the ego would convince you that to know Love, you must set up your world so that you never experience the challenges and the insecurities of abandonment, aloneness, not-knowingness. Hmm?

Where is my next meal coming from?

The attempt to create material security flows only from the egoic mind. For the *enlightened* mind is in *complete abundance, always.*

When I walked this world as a man, and was taught by the Essenes, I and my brothers and sisters learned to practice a way of life (that, by the way, is also known in other cultures, in what you call your ancient India) in which a conscious decision was made to give up all materiality, and to walk, literally, naked in the world owning nothing, possessing nothing, facing the stark reality of the body's perfect vulnerability [laughs], relying on the expressions of Grace and Love through others. Walking around with a begging bowl and simply saying,

The body-mind is hungry. Would you be so kind as to fill my bowl?

Receiving the "yes" or "no" with the *very same* appreciation.

Lesson Eight

Many of you listening to this tape have no idea what it means to be hungry. You think hunger is that temporary gnaw that occurs because you haven't gone to your refrigerator in the last few hours. Go and abide in the forest with nothing to eat. Take nothing with you but perhaps some water; and abide alone, open to the elements, for three days and three nights. And then, you will know *something* of what it means to be an Essene, to be one who goes without any attempt to protect the body-mind from the deepest fears of its own demise.

Once, a rich man came unto me and asked me to teach him. And I simply replied,

> *Go and sell all that you have and follow me.*

He didn't want God *that* much.

And again, of course, as I've said unto you many times, it doesn't mean you must go and give away your material wealth that you have in your world. It *does* mean you must give away your *attachment to it*. You must see that it is merely an illusion, that it cannot provide to you the safety that you truly seek. For safety can come only in reclining into the Heart of God.

> *The body-mind is not even mine. The mate is not mine. The career is not mine. The bank accounts are not mine. These things of the world* cannot *keep my soul safe. They* cannot *awaken me. Only my decision to surrender the world, to transcend the world, to abide as empty in the world, only my decision to teach only Love, can awaken me to the invulnerability beyond the vulnerability of all created things — even this very body-mind, that I once mistakenly identified with as my self.*

The truly Awakened come and go as the wind. You know not from whence They have come, and you know not where They are going. For They don't even know these things—how can you? But They listen to the Voice of Spirit. And Spirit is like the whisper of the winds: *Come . Go .Touch . Speak . Refrain . Leave . Abstain . Embrace . Eat . Fast . Pray . Dance .*

The One who abides in unobstructed feeling nature flows with that which comes from the depth of a perfectly still heart and mind, and dances while knowing stillness. For the body-mind that others see is no longer inhabited by the contraction of the ego. The Enlightened cannot be understood. They can only be appreciated by the Enlightened.

Who, then, will you choose to be this day, beloved friends — one who walks in the ordinary world, or One who walks in Heaven, side by side with their Creator? Will you walk this day in the world as one who has everything figured out? Or will you walk as One who, in perfect innocence, merely loves—and laughs and chuckles within at the great illusion of the drama of this world?

For this world arises and passes away in the twinkling of an eye. It is merely like dots on a screen that have created a temporary movie. Once the movie plays out, the screen remains as it has always been, until the next movie comes to town. Your consciousness is like that screen. It *witnesses* that which arises and passes away, even within the body- mind itself. Identify with that pure screen, the pure witness, the *spaciousness* that is wider than all universes. Notice that part of you that is simply aware of what is arising—a feeling, a thought, a word, a song heard, a car crash witnessed. It doesn't matter. Anything arising in the field of your experience arises in the *field* of this *spaciousness of awareness* which *is* God's gift to you as your *very existence.* For Pure Spirit *is* awareness itself. And that awareness can be fueled by the decision for Love or the belief in fear.

Lesson Eight

And so, indeed, beloved friends, the message of this hour is again quite simple. But if you have truly chosen to enact this year as *The Way of Knowing*, do not waste time. Look well — over the next thirty days — *deeply at the Truth* of what's been running you. What are the patterns that created the choices, the reactions, the responses, the rationalizations, the great words, the great seeking, the great striving — all of it! Look well, and perceive, and know that which was birthed from fear, no matter what it looked like. For indeed, the wolf can come in sheep's clothing. And where have you been a ravenous wolf, coming in sheep's clothing, with false smiles, in order to get another to give you what you believe you lack? Where have you refrained from Love? Where have you refused to become perfectly vulnerable? For it is only on the other side of that decision that your perfect *in*vulnerability arises.

You are Love and nothing else. In any moment that you behave, speak, or perceive yourself to be other than Love, *you* have used the power of your awareness to decide for that which would attempt to stand *against* the Kingdom of God. And *you* are the one that has suffered for it.

Love, indeed, beloved friends. So many of you that have heard my words through this, my beloved brother, look upon me with *such* great Love. You look upon me and go,

Oh, Jeshua. He just loves so perfectly!

Well, of course I do! Because I've come to see that there isn't anything else *worth doing!* I know that that sounds almost simplified, but the Truth *is* simple. *You* must come in your own Christed nature to see that in perfect innocence there isn't anything else to do but love — to love without limits, to love without fear, to love by extending perfect freedom to all of Creation to be and do what it wants to be and do. Then, and only then, can you know that nothing can betray you, nothing can hurt you, nothing can bring anything to you or take anything away. *You* have the infinite and perfect freedom to love! And in *that decision*, you know your Creator and can say, quite simply, with me,

> *Behold! I and my Father are one and the same! Now, let me give you a hug. Now let me set you free to have your experience. Now let me watch this great movie. Now let me enjoy my salad.*

It is all so, so very simple!

Never identify yourself with your *doing*, but let your *doing* be infused by your *being*. For while you're in the world, the body-mind *will* "do." It's very nature is action and activity itself. Just like it is the nature of a leaf in autumn to fall from a tree to the ground. Would you say,

> *Oh! Well, that shouldn't have happened! The leaf shouldn't have had to die. It shouldn't have had to change colors. Oh, what's wrong with this universe?*

You are like a leaf on the tree. And you are already falling to the moment of your death. How much more time will you *waste* before you decide to *break through the chains of fear* held in the very tissues of the body-mind? How much longer will you wait to enjoy the dance of the fall from the branch of birth to the ground of death of the body-mind in order to experience the total freedom of the fall?

And here, indeed, beloved friends, we come full circle. For the great *fall from grace*, the great dream of the *dream of separation*, must finally be embraced and lived with perfect Love, obstructing nothing, knowing that the very momentary experience of the body- mind, in a perfectly insane world, is

Lesson Eight

okay, because it is illusion. To resist illusion is to insist that the illusion is real. It is only in the full *embrace* of an illusion that the illusion *dissolves* before your eyes. Love sets all things free again.

Over the next thirty days, do only this: Dedicate and commit each moment of each day to teaching only Love. Take upon yourself the commitment to discipline the mind and the heart, *while* opening the body without obstruction. In each moment, set all beings free, by being only committed to Love. See how much joy you can experience by being the Lover of all Life.

Want nothing from no one. Need nothing from any one. Express your passion. Express your longing. Look upon the falling leaves, if they are happening in your neighborhood. Wherever you are, look upon all things and decide to *love the hell out of it*. For the hell in it is only what you have projected upon it. Take back your projection and embrace it with Love.

For thirty days — you can do it! For thirty days — such a small time frame in one human life! Would you not give yourself permission for thirty days — a three and a zero? This is not a difficult assignment! Anyone with any degree of intelligence and maturity can *surely* decide each morning, for one day, to teach only Love, and string thirty of them together!

If it is, in Truth, the transformation of your soul that you seek, so that only Christ is present where you are, complete this one assignment. And when it's done, simply do it again, and again, and again — worlds without end.

Heaven awaits you. Love waits on your welcome. And yet, that welcome is but the decision to finally *embrace yourself* and to live the Truth that has already set you free.

Love, and give all things complete freedom to be and to do as they will. For there is no other doorway to the perfect freedom that you have sought for oh, such a long, long time! Let time end, that eternity might be remembered. And only Love can set you free.

And indeed, with that, beloved friends, peace be unto you always. For indeed, it is *dripping* through the ethers of your very atmosphere, waiting for you to drink it in.

Peace be with you always.

Amen

Lesson Eight

PERSONAL NOTES

PERSONAL NOTES

Lesson Nine

Lesson Nine

Now, we begin.

And indeed, once again, greetings unto you, beloved and holy friends. As always, I come forth to abide with you because you have asked. As always, I come forth to abide with you because, in Truth, there is nowhere else that I could be. For where you are, I am. And where I am, you are. We abide, then, as the One Mind, birthed from the very Heart of *Abba*, or God. There is nothing outside of us. And from within, there is nothing hidden. Though the dimensions of Creation be infinite, they abide within the Mind, or the Field of Consciousness, that we share as One.

Because this is true — and I assure you that it is — there is, indeed, only one task which must be accomplished, one realization that must be realized, one Reality to be expressed and lived. And that simple Truth is that there is only One, that there is only Heaven, that there is only Love, that there is only the Perfect Peace that passes all understanding, that keeps, indeed, your hearts *in Mind*. For your heart, or your soul — that which is all that you have experienced throughout the multitude of your lifetimes upon this tiny planet, all of the experiences that you have garnered since before the beginning of time throughout all of the multitude of dimensions — the soul, or the heart, resides within the Mind of God, within the Mind of Christ; for these are One and the same.

Therefore, beloved friends, know always that the only Truth that must be lived, as you enter into the firm commitment of *choice*, to abiding in *The Way of Knowing*, is simply that there is only One Thing. You are That One. Your brother and your sister are That One. And though bodies come and go, though time seems to arise and pass away, though the dance of relationship, of career, of weather patterns, seems to come and go, it is only the *unenlightened mind* that looks for great signs in these things.

The Way of Knowing

In Truth, within the field of your soul, within all of the field of experiences that you call to yourself, the same gift is being offered. The gift offered to you, that by Grace you might decide to see that the world of ever-changing form means nothing — *the world means nothing*. It does not, nor has it *ever*, existed, except in the perceptions *conjured up* within the *field* of mind that seems to be particularly related to your soul. Now even that is a bit of an illusion.

But the point is simply this: In *The Way of Knowing*, there is a quiet decision to accept the Truth that is true always, to surrender, to open the palms of the hands and to release the tight grip upon the value, the meaning, and the *rightness* of the perceptions you have made to *veil* Reality. You are that Reality. All things are that Reality. The forms that the physical eyes show you arise and pass away. Yet, in each moment, Mind remains perfectly clear, perfectly One. Only the *spell* of the mind that believes itself to be the body creates suffering, creates doubt, creates illusion.

Wherever you are, then, in this very moment, you can *only* be where, in Truth, I am. Wherever *I* seem to be in this moment, I can *only be* where *you* are. For indeed, in *The Way of Knowing*, what must come to be released is the mistaken perception that there is, or has ever been, a separate "I" that is *localized* where the body-mind is.

To release this illusion is to see that all things are simply one thing: automobiles, plants, trees, clouds, thoughts arising and passing away. They appear in different forms, but they are but one thing. Looking through such an Enlightened Mind, because It no longer sees the veil of the false "I" standing between Itself as a filter and Its *recognition* of Its union with — Its identity with — all things arising and passing away . . . such a Mind looks out upon a transfigured world, a world in which the veil

Lesson Nine

has been lifted. And That Mind *sees* only Itself. It *sees* that the very things It had been judging as imperfect, as It looked out upon the world—that It had been judging through fear, that It had been judging through self-doubt—those very things, of themselves, are perfect; that they are, indeed, the Kingdom of Heaven.

This is why the distance between where you are and where I am is, indeed, a distance that cannot be measured. For, in Reality, there is no gap. In Reality, separation does not exist. In Reality, your *fall from Grace* and your movement into unenlightenment, itself has been but an illusion. The very life you have been living is *absolutely perfect*. The life you are living now is *absolutely perfect*. And it hasn't anything at all to do with where the body-mind goes. It has nothing to do with whether you watch a movie or read a book, whether you make money or do not, whether the body-mind lives or dies. The life you have been living is the life of awareness, of consciousness, of perfect freedom to create whatever perception you choose to hold. You are free, then, in all moments, to see that what has been arising as the Life of your very Self *is* the Life and Mind of God.

A Mind so awakened looks out and sees that there are no problems. Such a Mind looks out upon the world and sees no reason to change it, for It is now looking at a world that has *already* been *healed*, already been *transfigured*, already—through alchemical fires, if you will—been *purified* and made whole again. For, in Reality, It sees that that wholeness was *never once lost*. The dream of separation occurs within a space of mind that is nowhere, that holds no value and no purpose.

Fear, then, has no power over *you*. Death has no power over *you*. You abide, then, in the only place ever created for you. You are not localized to the body or the particular personality that you have associated with as your "I" — that, in itself, is part of the spell, or the drama, or the dream, of separation.

In *The Way of Knowing*, there is a simple and quiet decision to behold that — as the body-mind plays itself out, as the coming and going of all forms *around* you and *within* you, as your own unique perceptual field changes and dances and ebbs and flows (and we'll get to why it does that in just a moment), as all of these things that seem to be within you in your private world (and that's a bit of a misnomer) and in your external world (that you think is yours and not someone else's) — all of these things are innocent, harmless, they hold no power, and there is no Reality in them. And yet, they are Reality, Itself, when seen through eyes that are not identified with the false "I," with the localized sense of identity. Even the body-mind, that you once called your "self," is merely seen to arise and pass away in the vast expanse of your true Self, the Self that is shared by all beings in all dimensions — always.

It was this understanding that allowed me to simply choose to give myself over to what was called the crucifixion. An Enlightened Consciousness knows that loss is impossible. An Enlightened Consciousness knows that gain is also impossible. And yet, an Enlightened Consciousness, resting in the Certainty of Perfect Knowing, merely abides in Reality. That means there is no resistance to the coming and going of the body, no resistance to the grand display of energies that make up what you call your world. Governments rise and fall, a new model automobile is unveiled, to the flash of a thousand camera bulbs — some minds take it as being a very serious thing, some don't even notice — and *all* of it is *you*! All of it is arising in the vast expanse of the perfectly free Mind that belongs to no one, and yet, in which, all Ones arise.

Lesson Nine

An Enlightened Mind, then, whether it is experiencing — temporarily in the body-mind — sadness, joy, anger, guilt, hurt, ecstasy, lovemaking, a piece of fruit, cold wind on the skin . . . All of these things are merely allowed without resistance to be exactly what they are, while That Mind perceives and knows them to be harmless, vast, eternal, radiating the Light that God is.

For in Truth, in the end, as we come near the end of this year of *The Way of Knowing*, the Truth must be told ever more simply and ever more simply. There is only Reality. That Reality I have called *Abba*. That One is One *with* me, and I am That One. That One is One with *you*, and You *are* That One.

In the end, then, what seems to be *radical* to a world caught in the spell of the small self, seemingly playing its drama out through the field of many, many body-minds, the Truth does, indeed, become radical:

The Truth is that all that arises and passes away is, indeed, God. There is *only* God. There can *only be* God. And you are That.

For in the end, even the creative teaching device of God and Son, Creator and Created, begins to slip away, as duality becomes the One, as illusion — the last traces of illusion — finally give way to Truth.

All things that arise and pass away are perfectly okay. All opportunities to experience the awareness of *Love's presence* are okay. Every opportunity to experience the contraction of *fear* is okay. For these things arise *only in* the field of the perfectly free Mind that you are.

The Way of Knowing

So you see, in the end, it is not so much about cutting out certain experiences and having only certain ones that you've decided hold value. It is, rather, to see that *all* such experiences are transitory. A moment of ecstasy or a moment of sadness are *one and the same* for the Enlightened Mind. There is only that Vast Expanse that allows all things. And when *nothing* is any longer unacceptable to you, in the field of what seems to be your own unique, particular experience, you will know that you are Home. Things arise and pass away, and you remain.

Beloved friends, I Am indeed That One that birthed Christ. I Am indeed That One that walked this Earth as a man and manifested the fullness of Myself, to reveal Myself *to* Myself. You are That One that birthed Jeshua ben Joseph. You are That One that set in motion the great drama of the dream of separation and its correction. You are, indeed, That One, that alone exists unchanging, unchangeable, and unchanged forever.

And yet, when the mind has been under the spell of thoroughly believing it is a separate body-mind, and that body is, indeed, the source of the "spell" that creates the illusion of a localized, separate self, a soul that has no connection to anyone else or anything else . . . In the field of the body-mind, if I were to have come to you three, four, five, ten, two thousand years ago and said,

> You are, alone, That One. You are God and only God exists,

your fear, already present, would have been heightened. And so I came to you in the guise of a man known as Jeshua ben Joseph. I played out a perfectly clear *drama*, like so many body-minds. I allowed Myself to be perceived as a unique individual, since *you* believed that unique individuals exist.

Lesson Nine

You saw Me as separate from you. And so I appeared in the way that you could see Me and understand Me. And I have gone on, without ceasing, to appear in ways that you can see Me and understand Me, to speak in languages and words, metaphors and parables, teaching tools that you could receive without *increasing* your illusion of fear. All teaching devices, then—and in this guise even the appearance of Myself as Jeshua ben Joseph, was but a temporary teaching tool.

All teaching and communication devices have one, simple goal: To reduce fear so that that particular mind can release its grip on *itself* and surrender the illusion of separation and thereby, be bathed in the Light of Reality yet again—seeing that It is What I Am. And I Am God. I AM Abba. You Are God. You Are Abba. Only That One Exists. Only the "I" that We share as One exists.

I appear as every blade of grass. I appear as every thought. I appear as every desire. I appear as every cloud in the sky. I appear as You. You *are* That One that I Am. I Am speaking to you, and yet, You are speaking to You. You hear Me, but you hear only Yourself.

Understand well, then, that I, as Jeshua ben Joseph, Am but the appearance of God in a particular form, so that you could come closer to the Truth of Your Nature without recoiling in fear. It is, indeed, said in the Bible that,

> *No man looks upon the Face of God and lives.*

That statement means simply that the mind that is not yet enlightened, therefore living in fear, living in the perception of itself being separate from God, cannot look upon the *Face* of God, the *Reality* of God, and *live*. It was not a fearful statement at all. It was simply the Truth. For when the mind looks and beholds,

> *There is only God and I Am That,*

the *false self* has, indeed, died. Where did it go? Nowhere. Because it *never existed* in the first place. And that which closes the gap, though it may be said to you in many forms, is the *decision* to give up seeking and acknowledge that you have found.

All teaching devices, all forms of language that I have brought forth have been by design to *woo* you, to *seduce* you, to *calm* you into *Knowing* that You Are God. And the final gap then is, indeed—the final step—is taken *by Me*. And that final step taken by Me is the final step taken *by You*. For that final step into the fullness of enlightenment can only be *God recognizing that only God Is*. And *You Are That*.

Where else could we come to in such a series of tapes, entitled *The Way of Knowing*? By *Way of Knowing*, it was never intended to be a set of lessons that will someday *get you there*, but rather the very *Way* of Knowing—to walk the journey of Creation, *Knowing* that it is God doing the walking . . . To walk in the Knowingness that all things that arise inhere in God, and You Are That . . . To finally be willing to look at a tree and Know that the Eye of God is seeing God, and the Tree of God is being eyed by God.

You are, indeed, That One, infinite, eternal, unbounded, so intimately linked with every one of your brothers and sisters that there is no such separation, nor anything to fear. And there is yet this infinitely magical process in which *Mind* is realized within a body-mind. That is, *you* can be perfectly enlightened *now*, by simply seeing the Truth that the thought you have held of yourself has never been true. It was only a temporary spell—

Lesson Nine

God forgetting, God playing to be other than God. And yet, that play is the very fullness of God. For in the end, the "fall from Grace," the *separation from union*, by whatever term you choose to use it, that very thing, *itself*, cannot be outside the Mind of God.

All that your eyes show you is innocent and free. All that the mind can conjure as thought is innocent and free. You are free to be That One who as the Mind of Christ—which, by the way, is God—shows up in the transfigured body-mind. Where once there was a false sense of "I," now there is only the free, unobstructed Field of Awareness of God observing Creation *through* His Creation . . . God observing His Creation *through* His Creation.

Imagine, then, that you are, indeed, That One, and *you* choose to pick up a particular body-mind that everyone *thought* was called Fred or Nancy or Harry or what have you. You put on the body-mind for the simple enjoyment of looking out through it to observe what Creation is like from that perspective. Not unlike one who would go to a costume ball, puts on a certain costume just to *play* at being Louis the Fourteenth or Lady Godiva; Mother Mary. Or, if you want to be very radical, Jesus of Nazareth.

You have already put on all of those costumes. You are the Creator of all of those costumes. You Are God. There is *only* God. There can only *be* God. And as you listen to sounds vibrating through the air, through your tape machine—the machine, the vibration, the words, the insights and pictures that are flowing through the field of the mind, the "you" who is listening and the "I" who is speaking are all One Thing: God.

Fear not then, beloved friends. Fear not the coming and going of the life of the body-mind. For that life, in itself, is already perfectly unobstructed and free. It *cannot* hinder the Truth of who you are when you choose to see *from* the Truth of *what* you are. Dare then, as we begin to conclude this year of *The Way of Knowing*, to live, what is this called in your world, the "impossible dream." Dare to begin to see that You are God, perceiving—looking out upon—God's Creation. And God's Creation is only God!

Yes, in the end, you can even say that God has created nothing. For nothing can be *outside* of what God Is. I have given unto you many clues over the years. I have told you that if God forgot to think about you for one moment, you would cease to be. Think about what that must mean. It *must* mean that you are inhering so much in God, that a simple thought in the Mind of God both creates you or destroys you. In the flash of an eye, you either are in existence or you are not. And yet, what could then be in existence *but* the Will of God? If you *exist*, you *must be* in the Mind of God—that Perfect Power by which all things arise and pass away.

And God's Creation occurs nowhere. That is, It has no location. The planet Earth, the bodies that inhabit it, the physical universe in which the planet Earth is spinning about—all of these things are not at all unlike what you experience when you close your eyes and imagine having ice cream. You create the image. You have the experience. You see yourself giving the cashier your golden coins (or in this case, perhaps, some of your silver coins). You eat the ice cream. You see yourself smile. You can feel it move down into your belly. Where did all of that exist? Could anybody find it outside the power of consciousness to create? No.

Lesson Nine

You are like the ice cream in the Mind of God. God sees Himself, appearing as you, doing exactly what you are doing in each and every moment. And if God, *for one split second*, dropped the thought of you, you would entirely disappear. And all of those beings around you, who you think are different people, would instantly have no recollection of you, whatsoever.

There can only be God. You are God's Dream. You are God's Creation. You are God's *Child*, in the sense that you are God shaping Itself into a temporary expression of Itself. And for what purpose? To simply extend Creation. You *are* That One! *All Power under Heaven and Earth resides within you!* When you bend to pick up a glass, God is embracing God! And if God were not choosing that, in that moment, you would cease to be. Even the body would vanish from view.

As Jeshua ben Joseph, then, I have appeared to you to be your brother and friend, because *you* have believed that you needed some *one* to be a brother and friend, who will let you know that you are safe so that you can give yourself permission to nod your head yes, and say,

> *I can accept that now. Thank you for being here, Jeshua.*

And yet, in Truth, you are God merely playing out that field of relationship, the quality of experience that seems to require an elder brother who has gone through quite a change and now has the voice of authority.

But I have no voice unless you give it to me. And what can give such authority, if not the Mind of God? For it takes One to know One. You have heard me say that many, many times. It can only be the Christ Mind *in you* that could perceive the Christ Mind in Jeshua ben Joseph. And the Christ Mind *is* the extension of

The Way of Knowing

God's Perfect Being into, and as, Creation.

When you look lovingly upon anyone, *You are God*. For God is but Love. You have heard me say many times, Love is the essence of what You are. If God is Love, and Love is the essence of what You are, this can only mean that the essence of You *is* God—right here, right now, with not one thing that must be done to *earn* it, to *shape* it, to *get* it. This is why no form of technique brings the Son to the Father.

This is why I once said, even through this my beloved "Son," if you will, in what was called once, *The Jeshua Letters*—again, only a teaching device given to those who could accept Me in the guise of Jeshua ben Joseph, for you had already decided to give Me authority to guide you through that form—this is why I said unto you that no prayer or supplication brings the Son to the Father, but only in the release of illusion. And that illusion, when you've peeled it all down in the way that you have insisted on peeling it down, is to come to see that the notion you have held of yourself, as having a separate existence, being a separate "I," has been false. It is a smoke screen, a guise, a veil. Your perception or belief that that is what you were, as opposed to being everything else, is the illusion that must be released.

And in *The Way of Knowing*, what I am offering to you as, indeed, your Creator, and the Essence of All that You Are, is the opportunity to choose this context to decree that only God exists, that the very body-mind and the self you once thought you were is now embodied, inhabited by, the Creator, Itself. That when the hand moves to pick up the glass, it is no longer "I," but God; no longer "me," as a separate struggling being, but God who *moves* the hand, God who is *aging* the hand, and God who is *the aging* of the hand. *All things* can only be That which I Am.

Lesson Nine

I Am One and singular and whole and you should have no other gods before Me, no other thoughts or illusions before Me, not even a sense of an "I" going to God. Then there is only God. And Reality has descended to make Its home in the Field of Awareness where once you thought there was something else. We have enjoined with you to create *The Way of The Heart*, to begin to speak in such a way to you that would not elicit fear, to which you could nod your head and say,

Yes, yes. That sounds true to me. I'll accept this.

And then, we spoke to you of *The Way of Transformation*, where you perceived yourself as one in *need* of transformation. And, again, you nodded your heads and said,

We'll accept this. Yes, I am a sinful creature, still in need of transformation. I'll buy into this as the context in which I receive more of the Truth about myself.

And in *The Way of Knowing*, which is now, we begin to bring you, full force, into that which you have chosen to bring yourself to — to stand at the doorway of the Temple of Heaven, to begin to open it, to let the Golden Light stream out.

And as you look into that sanctuary to see, it is *Yourself* upon the throne. This is why I have also said that Self-love — *Self-love* — is that doorway that brings about the release of illusion; the simplicity of Self-love. This does not mean that you just hang out in a state of consciousness that says,

Well, I'm really kind of a weak being, but I accept and love myself.

That's a good beginning. But eventually you must say,

I Am God and I love Myself. I Am That One abiding as the leaf that falls from the tree. I Am, indeed, That One that shudders against the cold of a winter storm. I Am, indeed, That One that is the warmth of the sunlight that comes to caress the flower. I Am the flower that receives the sunlight. I Am this body-mind arising and passing away. I Am the quality of awareness that I choose, now!

For there is only God. Only the Truth can be true. And the Truth sets *all things free*. For if Truth is given only to mankind, but not to a blade of grass, the blade of grass remains imprisoned. But the Truth that sets all things free does so because *all things are the Truth*.

This is why, when you encounter *anyone*, it is, indeed, a *holy* encounter. "Holy" means *wholeness*. In wholeness there is only One.

So, I hope you are beginning to see how simple it really is. Each moment of relationship is "holy," not because the mind decides to hold the thought,

Well, I heard this was holy. I guess I better be a nice person.

No! That's egoic thinking, and the ego *is* the dream of separation. Who is dreaming the dream? You are. And You Are God.

Each relationship, or each moment, is a "holy encounter" because there is only *wholeness* showing up as that One Thing. Existence is not really two beings coming together and having an experience. There is only the One Thing which is the Experience Itself. Do you know that, all along, you have never forgotten Me for a moment?

Lesson Nine

That is, in any moment of *true perception*—true, clear, immediate perception—you have been unaware of the thought of an "I" having the experience. There is just the experience itself. It arises innocently. It arises uncaused. There is no judgment about it. There is just experience.

Then, in the next millisecond (snaps fingers), the next slight moment, you create the thought,

> *Oh! I am having this experience and it's with that separate being over there.*

You have merely elected to use the Power of God Consciousness to identify that another body-mind is something separate from you. You Are the Creator of the game. You Are the players in the game. You Are the result and consequences of the game. You Are the end of the game. And You Are That in which all games disappear as though they had never been.

This means, beloved friends, look around you. The world is not outside of you at all. It *is* you. You are playing a game. That game is going to take this very planet into a transfiguration in Light. And you will all be transformed in the twinkling of an eye (laughing). Well, of course you will be. You Are God making up the game.

That's all that's going on. That's all that's ever been going on. There is only That which I Am. There is only That which *I Am*. I Am, indeed, that Perfect Impersonal I. I Am the Creator of all things, the Sustainer of all things, the Destroyer of all things.

There has never been a separate "I" where you are. There has only been Me, showing up as You. You are perfect and whole, and you are innocent. You have never failed and you have never sinned. How could these things be, that I have spoken to you, time and time again, as Jeshua ben Joseph, unless you are already whole? And wholeness is God. You are It. You are the destination of all your seeking.

In the beginning, the Mind—which is Me, which is God, pretending to be separate—plays Itself out and tries to make Itself be as separate as It thinks It can be. But separation *never* succeeds. The first step in the awakening process is to *hear the word*. You will hear the word (and everyone listening to these tapes has, indeed, heard the word) when *you* decide, as God, to have the experience of being a being awakening to the Truth. And the word will be given unto you in a form that you choose. Everyone listening to these tapes chose to hear the word through Me as Jeshua ben Joseph.

That vibration, received by you, set you on your course toward perfect remembrance and enlightenment. You are the one that created the drama of the crucifixion. You are the One that set in motion the return of Jeshua ben Joseph as the primary teacher in this world. Why? Because you are That One that has decreed that it is this context in which you will give yourself permission to edge ever closer to the Reality that the *whole thing* is God, and You Are That.

What has been playing out, then, for these past three years of these tapes, and even longer than that—indeed, been playing out for two thousand years—is Your Creation. The Game of God, remembering God, through the guise of God's Creation.

Lesson Nine

As you come, then, to accept a savior, or a teacher, or a teaching, that is a *stage* in the awakening process. When you decide to release your grip of fear a little deeper, you begin, then, to have what are called *mystical experiences*. You begin to realize that you can be aware of someone else, not in the room with you physically. You begin to have unique and extraordinary experiences (laughing) of communicating with beings that don't have bodies. And oh, my goodness, it all looks to be so *incredible*! And yet, even that is but a stage of the journey.

And as the mind becomes more and more transparent to itself, the more it is simply choosing to release illusion and abide in Reality, it *must come* to the door of the Temple of Heaven. It must open that door, which is to release any final sense of being outside the Sanctuary of Truth. It must come to be basked in the Light that flows from the Source and Essence of All That Is. And the separate seeker, the one who would know God, realizes that they already know God perfectly. And that they have indeed been God, seeking God, for the enjoyment of finding and knowing God, again.

Yes, that is your challenge now. *Would you be willing to simply be God?* Do you know what that requires? *Absolutely nothing.* How then, do you show up as God? If you are thirsty, drink your water. If it is cold, put a sweater on. If you want to make love, make love. If you want to sleep, sleep. There is no difficulty in this. The only practice is to *be that which You Are and You Are the Light of the world*. How many times have you heard me say that to you?

Be that which You Are and You Are the Light of the world. You have heard the words and said,

Oh, now if I could only be who I Am, then I'd be the Light of the world. But I'm not being who I Am, so I must be the darkness of the world.

But the whole time, you are, indeed, being who You Are. You Are the Light that lights the world. For in being whatever you've chosen to be at any moment, You Are That which generates awareness of experience. And that is all that We Are as the Mind of God: *That which generates experience*. For experience *is* the extension of Creation.

You have not failed in separating yourself from your Self. You have not succeeded in shaking the hand off of your own arm. The joke has been on you, because you wanted to be "joked." *In each moment of your existence, you have been the perfect expression of God.* Even in the moments of your deepest so-called suffering, when you believed that everybody else had it and you didn't, when you perceived yourself as being light-years from knowing God, you were the very *Power* of God creating that perception.

You are also That One who has *dared* to be *bold* enough to allow Shanti Christo into your life — a rather radical organization. You created it as the context for your awakening. And you are free to use that context, that organization, to enlighten the entire planet, if you want to. You are also free to let it crumble into an ancient echo of memory. There is only God, and You Are That.

God extends Creation without ceasing. You will, therefore, *always* continue to exist as The One who creates experience. And this is why there is only one question worth asking,

> What do I truly want?

Lesson Nine

For you will experience the answer to that question. And, in fact, your experience *is* the answer to the question. You can lay in bed with the flu and ask yourself the question,

> *What do I truly want? Well, this body-mind has the flu. I am experiencing exactly what I have wanted.*

And you can embrace it and love it, and see it as perfectly innocent, because that is the Truth of it. Having the flu is not a sign of failure. The death of the body is not a sign of failure. It's just what is arising as the extension of Creation.

And so, the final and greatest Truth that can be told sounds like complete nonsense! It is *unacceptable* to the egoic mind that wants the power of *making* the false, separate self-all-powerful and invincible, standing against the world — in other words, the gnat shouting at the universe. For the Mind that is awakened to the Reality of God allows all things, trusts all things, embraces all things, transcends all things, and sees the shimmering perfection literally showing up as all things.

You are perfectly free in every moment. Nothing can imprison God. If you choose to *leave* a relationship, you are merely using the complete freedom of God to generate experience. If you choose to *stay* in a relationship, you are merely using the freedom of God to generate experience. Neither is right. Neither is wrong. Both options are totally free and uncaused. And *each* expresses God. It is, indeed, time to give up perceiving some things as being more perfect than others. There is only God. There has only been God. There will always be only God.

When a wave is cast up out of the ocean, it does not lose its wetness. And who would say that *this* wave is better than *that* wave? And yet, I say unto you, the mind that chooses one wave over the other *is* the Mind of God creating Creation. For in the very moment when one wave is chosen as having a greater value, *experience* has been had. And experience *is* the extension of Creation. You, therefore, *are* a Creator, and you create *without ceasing*. And you remain, today, exactly as you were when you were created by your Self.

You remain free to create whatever you want to perceive. And you do it from within the mind and you extend it out, you radiate it out, with every thought you think. When an Enlightened Master shows up on the planet, it is simply that God has given up playing the game of the separate self through that body-mind. That's all. An Enlightened Mind realizes that there is only God, and that in that freedom, it is free to show up as the body-mind in whatever way It wants, while the body-mind lasts. Whether It shows up with saffron robes or a beggar's worn-out clothing makes no difference. An Enlightened Mind is an Enlightened Mind. It might smoke a cigarette. It might drink carrot juice. It becomes irrelevant. And the one smoking the cigarette looks at the one drinking the carrot juice and smiles. The one drinking the carrot juice looks at the one smoking the cigarette and smiles. And in that smile, there is only The One, beholding The One.

You, then, are free to be at peace. You are, then, free to release all judgment. You are, indeed, free to give yourself the exquisite experience of being The One who allows all things. You are The One who is free to embrace the innocence of each moment. You are The One who is free to require sunglasses against the morning sunrise. You are The One who is free to be *free*. And to be free is to be *authentic*. And to be authentic is to *demonstrate* the Reality that only God exists.

For those of you that have looked upon that which I have called, in one guise, "this My beloved brother," and in another guise,

Lesson Nine

"this My Beloved Son," if you would go back and read *The Jeshua Letters*, not all of those communications were from the perspective of Jeshua ben Joseph. There was also direct communication from the Mind of God, given as a clear and obvious *sign* unto you. Things were said even in that book, that revealed the Truth that there is only God. If you looked past it and did not see it, it is because you still thought it would be too fearful for you to know the Truth that sets you free. And you needed to perceive that there was an individual, name Jon Marc, who had an experience opening to Jeshua ben Joseph, and that you are receiving information through the medium of a channel. And yet, I say unto you, you have received information only from your Self: God.

Therefore, the transformation that you perceive in this one that you would think to be a self-separate from you, named Jon Marc, is merely a body-mind in which only the Mind of God exists. That Mind operates the body-mind to teach the Truth to you, and You are God choosing to remember that You are God. This is why all giving is receiving. This is why loss is not possible, and why death does not exist. God can only dissolve into God. And in that realization, *the final step*, the final step beyond *The Way of Knowing* (there's a clue for you), beyond even *The Way of Knowing*, is to release resistance to Creation, Itself, and learn to show up as God in individuated form—to have a good time: to love, to create, to extend.

Therefore, indeed, beloved friends, Our Love will be without ceasing. Our creativity will be without ceasing. For We Are, indeed, That One showing up *as* Creation for the *joy of the dance*. There is nothing but this. There is nothing above or below, nothing behind or ahead. You Are indeed That One *now*. And if you rest upon your couch with eyes closed, Who's doing the resting? Whose Eyes are closed? Hmm.

And so, already in this short message, I have given unto you the very rock-bottom, most fundamental core that you can now sit with—or dance with—if you wish. You can take it to bed with you. You can have a cup of coffee with it. You can *strive* to *understand* it. You can analyze it, saying,

> Well, there must be some secret message here. This must be metaphor, somehow.

Or you can simply give up being identified as a separate self still struggling to know the Truth.

In *A Course in Miracles*, I said unto you,

> Holy relationship is when any two have looked within and found no lack, and therefore choose to join to create, to make happy.

If any two have looked within and found no lack, they have seen that there is only God. Who cares whether this body-mind goes there or this one goes over there? It's all the same. Where do you feel like playing? That's all.

And when you see your brother or sister say, I am moving from this location to that location, the Awakened Mind says,

> Oh, this is a part of my Self wanting to go live in Cleveland now—perfectly okay.

For the Enlightened Mind gives perfect freedom to all beings because it sees that the expression of all beings is the freedom of its own Self, of the One Mind which is God, showing up as that being who would rather take the body-mind to Cleveland instead of living in Florida.

A totally Enlightened Mind says to the lover who awakens at three in the morning and says,

Lesson Nine

I now need to move to a monastery and live in perfect silence in a solitary cell. I will never see you again,

the Enlightened Mind receives that and smiles. For that Enlightened Mind knows that the lover can never truly leave, because separation is unreal. Therefore, the Enlightened Mind allows all things, trusts all things, embraces all things and transcends all things.

There is only God. And You Are That. You Are as I Am.

The only question, left, then is: *Who do you want to play with?* Who do you want to play with — Knowers of God or knowers of fear? They're all God. And yet in that play and display of Creation, you are free to decide who you will play with, who you will dance with, who you will create with, and *what* you will create. As any Mind awakens to Itself as God, It becomes more and more interested only in being with others who are like- Minded. It can no longer tolerate unenlightenment. Why? Because it's not as much fun. It's not as loving. And God Is but Love.

Therefore, indeed, beloved friends, listen well to what has been shared with you this hour. And if you have been noticing, quite a shift has just occurred. The "cat is out of the bag." For Jeshua ben Joseph has been but a guise, a disguise, chosen of Me to present Myself to you, because you have *required it.*

Indeed, beloved friends, be at peace always. Let us play together as that One Mind, extending Creation without end, inviting aspects of Our Self back to Our Self. Only Love is Real. Only Love exists. Only Love is worthy of Love. And God wants only that which extends the *good,* the *holy,* and the *beautiful.* Therefore, indeed, peace be with you always (laughing). For in Truth, where could it go?

Go then in peace, beloved friends, and *Know*: I Am with you always.

Amen.

Lesson Nine

PERSONAL NOTES

The Way of Knowing

PERSONAL NOTES

Lesson Ten

Lesson Ten

Now, we begin.

And, indeed, once again, greetings unto you, beloved and holy friends. I — we come forth to abide with you because, again, you have asked. You have asked that That One that we have called *Abba* appear through His created forms as I, Jeshua ben Joseph, as we, which we will call here "the Lineage," and also through this, my beloved brother, who serves, yet, in the physical world as the physical conduit of that Wisdom, of that Energy that, in Truth, the Father Is.

The Father Is what You Are. Therefore, *you* have asked to be guided into the recognition that only God exists, by sending forth a prayer unto me, and unto this Lineage, and unto your Creator, to appear unto you in a *graded way*, that is, in a *slowly emerging way* that does not elicit an increase of fear. And yet, in Truth, your prayer has been to desire the awakening from the dream of the small self into the Reality that there has been nothing *but* God and You *Are* That. Therefore, indeed, beloved friends, as That One created and birthed from the Mind of Abba, even as you are created and extend the Love of God in the realm of form, I come forth as your brother and your friend. And yet, only God exists.

I will be with you always, even unto the end of all *worlds*, that is, unto the end of all *illusions*. From that moment, Creation will extend Itself, with perfect *clarity*, with perfect *transparency*, as God merely extends God in a joyous, ecstatic act of becoming the forms of Creation, merely to celebrate and praise God. For the very purpose of all created forms of consciousness is to *express* praise of the Creator.

It is impossible to extend praise of the Creator without *fully* loving oneself. Without embracing and loving the particular manifestation of *God as you*, you cannot *fully* step into the complete expression of the praise of the Creator. Therefore, you have heard me say unto you many times, that the veil that keeps you from the Kingdom is the lack of self-love. Self-love is *essential* to return to the Kingdom. For self-love *is* the Love of the Creator. You cannot love the Creator while rejecting the Creator's Creation.

Indeed, then, beloved friends, know well that we who would come unto you, indeed, we that *have* been coming unto you since the day, and hour, and moment that this work began some twelve years or so ago—from the very moment I first appeared in the mind of this, my beloved brother—it has always been a "we" and not just an "I," as Jeshua ben Joseph. For there are, indeed, many of us who are linked together, in what we call "the Lineage," that extends far back in your history of time, creating what you might call in your scientific terms a *resonance of energy* that links the Mind of the Creator, through the epochs of time, through many individual minds, even unto this moment.

It is, indeed, that Lineage that brought forth the strand of salvation that culminated in my incarnation as Jeshua ben Joseph. The script was written thousands of years before. The linkages of energy were created generation unto generation unto generation unto generation, culminating in the birth of me as a man who opened to the Reality of Abba as the *only* Reality, through which the Creator could extend the Perfect Love of Himself and make it *visible* to His Children abiding in the spell, or under the spell, of illusion.

That work has never ceased. And, indeed, let it be known that the work that is done through this, called the Shanti Christo, is an extension of, and a collaboration with, the entirety of that Lineage, that strand of Light, extending from the Mind of God into the forms of time with *one purpose*—to *awaken* every aspect

Lesson Ten

of the Sonship. And what can the Sonship be but the extension of God into form, into that which appears as an individual — that which can create, that which can enter into holy relationship, that which can remember the fullness of Abba, *while* being the particular individual in the field of space and time.

The purpose, then, of the Lineage has never changed. And it has, indeed, gained in power through practice and through *adding* to its numbers. Imagine, then, a *field of energy* that attracts minds floating by it. And as those minds begin to resonate with the message or the word of God, as it is being expressed through this energy field, this Lineage, they become like unto the field of energy itself. As one of us once said, and is still recorded in your Bible,

> *Let that mind be in you which was also in the one we have chosen to call our Lord, the one known as Jeshua ben Joseph, or the Christ.*

When Paul wrote those words, he was referring to just this process in which you, under the spell of separation, release the spell, begin to resonate with the Mind of the Christ, begin to take up your seat within this expanding Lineage of Light — a direct descendant, a direct Disciple of God.

Therefore, indeed, beloved friends, understand well the role that you play wherever you are upon this plane. You may be living in a farmhouse with very few neighbors. You might be living in a — what do you call these? — the condominiums in your New York City. And yet, wherever you are, you are about something *extraordinary*. You are about that process whereby, from the moment the tiny mad, serious thought of separation was dreamed . . . you are about the very process through which the Creator is *correcting* the illusion of separation.

The Way of Knowing

There is nothing occurring upon your planet that is not about that. It either expresses separation, or it extends the *correction* of separation. There is only Heaven or the *illusion* of hell. Therefore, understand that you are an extraordinary being. You, right where you are, are given opportunities, moment to moment, to be the Truth of who you are, and therefore, be the Light that lights the world. You are part of an ancient Lineage that stretches back to before Creation began. That strand of Light has never been broken or lost.

I, as Jeshua ben Joseph, am merely the culmination of the expression of That in the field of space and time. And from that moment it has begun to spread out and to seep, if you will, into more and more minds, as the Sonship is awakened to the resonance with the Field of Energy that is the Christ Mind. *You are in the process of ultimate transfiguration.* You are part of an ancient Lineage with but one purpose: the complete transfiguration of human consciousness into being the literal field of *Christ Mind*, extending Creation throughout the physical dimension.

There are many extraordinary things ahead for humanity. There are many extraordinary things ahead for *you*. And no matter how deeply you have stepped into this journey, no matter how many transfigurative experiences you have had, as the false self melts away, and the Reality of Abba is birthed in the Mind made by God, there is always more. *There is always more.* For the Father never ceases in extending Himself into the forms of His Creation—*never*. That which the soul *is*, even beyond the life span of the body, the soul can never die. Nor will it ever be *completed*. For Creation is an infinite process of extending the *good*, the *holy*, and the *beautiful*.

Lesson Ten

Understand well, then, that you are not an ordinary person. You no longer walk this planet asleep. You may have thoughts saying,

> *I'm still not there. I still don't quite get this* Way of Knowing. *Uh! That takes my breath away to hear there's only God, and I am That!*

Let it take your breath away! Enjoy the experience, knowing that *that is* precisely the most perfect thing that can be occurring in the process of transfiguration that *you* are undergoing.

You are already *in* the Hands of Abba. You are already embraced and supported by many, many beings, abiding in a nonphysical dimension, that are part of this expanding circle of energy that we call "the Lineage." Our numbers are numerous. Many of our *names*, if you will, are known to you. Who are we, then? Well, you know me. You know that of Germain. You know that of Mary. You know that of Abraham and Moses. There are many, many others. You know the names of the prophets of the Torah.

The entire Lineage, then, expressed Itself down through the birthing of what is called the Jewish Nation, which carries the great strand of the Messiahship, culminating in the birth of me, Jeshua ben Joseph. You are part of a *very* ancient Family.

You are becoming one and the same as that *field of shimmering, radiant Light* that is the Purity of the Love of God shining through consciousness into the realm of matter, if you will, into the physical dimension.

This makes you not ordinary, but *extraordinary*. For without fanfare and without external ritual, which often casts only a spell over the heart and mind (the ego loves ritual), you have,

The Way of Knowing

indeed, gone through many *initiations*. The day and the hour in which you first opened to me, through this particular form of communication, through this my beloved brother, you underwent an initiation. You gave your *consent* to your Creator to *transfigure your beingness* so that it becomes the conduit through which the Creator extends Himself. And God is but Love. God is the Wisdom of the Christ Mind. God is the Sonship.

I want to, then, invite you in this hour, again in the *Way of Knowing*, to Know, to accept wholly, that *you are in extraordinary company*. You are not sleepwalking on the planet any longer. You have already begun to see beyond illusions, to penetrate what your eyes used to tell you were just the form and dance of matter and molecules, personas and egos and bodies. You have begun to see the *invisible strand*, the *invisible dance*, that is truly going on. You have begun to have visions and dreams. You have begun to feel inspired. You have begun to learn *forgiveness*, *healing*, and even *self-love*.

Self-love, then, is the *perfection* of all spiritual practice. Self-love *is* the final, shining Ray of Light that illuminates the heart of the individuated Ray of Light that you are. Self- love transfigures the mind, the emotional body, and even the physical body, to the degree that it strongly shines into the cells of the body.

Therefore, indeed, beloved friends, as we enter into these last days of this *Way of Knowing*, we have come in this hour to share with you that we do not so much come to a culmination, or an end, but to a *springboard* for what shall be. In these three years, we have sought to help you dismantle your illusions, to soften your heart and your mind, to be more and more willing to be *less fearful*. By becoming less fearful, you have, indeed, opened more and more to the guidance of the Holy Spirit.

Lesson Ten

Every choice for Love has been the result of a transfiguration that has been going on in the alchemy of your soul. You are an extraordinary being. You have been initiated into the strand of Light that we would here call that of the *Lineage*, the *Sacred Family*, dedicated to the manifestation and the fulfillment of the Atonement: *the awakening of the Sonship as the Mind of Christ.*

All that you do, in each moment, when you dedicate yourself to Love—again, whether you be living in a farmhouse or in a condominium in New York—adds to the field of energy being created that will one day tip the balance and dissolve *all* illusions from *all* minds. Your Life, then, is a Life in service to the Sonship, *regardless of the forms* in which you find yourself living. Your only task, then, is to decide, each day, to *surrender* anew, *desire* the Atonement, *intend* the Atonement, *allow* transfiguration to occur, *surrender* into the Truth:

> *Abba, you are the only thing that exists. Therefore, it makes no sense even to say, "Not my will, but Thine," for Yours, alone, Is. How shall we spend this one day?*

Each experience that you go through is the reshuffling of the cards, so to speak, as your life changes, and ebbs and flows, and miracles begin to come. Old friends go, new friends come. Hmm? All of it is the process whereby *your particular expression of Abba* is being transfigured into the Power and Purity of Christ.

We are with you wherever you go. The second thing that I wish to share with you this day is that *the power of the Lineage is available to you*. For in the first moment you chose to listen to me speak through this, my beloved brother, you entered through the *portal of an initiation*. And transfiguration has continued from that moment, to the degree you've been willing to allow it. In that moment, you—let us use something from your

The Way of Knowing

world—you've been "plugged into the circuitry" of the Lineage.

I want, then, to invite you in this hour's taping, to recognize that it is not just Jeshua ben Joseph who has manifested the fullness of the Christ Mind, but there are a *host*, a Heavenly host ... that's where all that language came from within the Jewish Torah and even the New Testament, taken over, by the way, by something called, "Christianity," which is not something I know much about, since I am, indeed, or was as a man, a Jew. But beyond that, I am of that strand of Light, expressing Itself through the tradition of the Jewish Family. And all of this has been by perfect design of Abba.

It is not the only strand. There are others—yes—universal strands that encompass the entirety of human experience. All souls have their lineage. There are strands expressed through that which is called India. There are strands expressed through that which is called, now, the Tibet. There are strands or lineages that extend themselves through the South Americas. There are strands or lineages that have extended themselves through the North American Indian. Do you see?

All of these strands are like spokes emanating from the hub of one wheel, reaching out to the farthest reaches of the dream of separation, attracting and calling the Sonship back together. So that whether one is Incan or Mayan or Anasazi or Tibetan or Indian or Jewish, or even if you're from New York, you are beginning to become part and parcel of One Mind that recognizes the Reality of the *invisible* permeating the realm of the *visible*. You are, indeed, taking up your place at the *right hand* of God. You know the phrase in your language "the right-hand man" (or the right-hand woman). It means *one who is in alignment, and acts only to fulfill the will of the one in charge*. It is a beautiful phrase, and it expresses *right-mindedness*.

Lesson Ten

Therefore, indeed, understand well, beloved friends, even if you are eighty-five years old, sitting in your comfortable rocking chair, believing that your life is just about to end, it can never end. The body-mind will be put to the dust of the ground, but you have already entered into a *fast track*. You are, indeed, a *mystic*. You are, indeed, going through the process of *transfiguration*, and *you are adding to the power of this Lineage*, to bring about the restoration of Heaven on Earth, and the re-establishment of the Christ Mind throughout the Sonship. And even when the body drops, let us just say that you will be "assigned to a new office" — that's all.

You — *you* listening to these words — are of *infinite importance* in the expression of this work that is called Shanti Christo. More, then, than an organization, and much more than a sacred piece of land to which many, someday, will come and will be healed — that is, will enter into the Christ Mind, just by the power of stepping into the *vortex of Purity* that has been established there. *You are already in that process.* As that Purity is established in you, you are, literally, affecting the creation and extension and expansion of the vortex on that land that has existed for a *very* long time. It is a portal, a doorway — there are many names that can be used — that takes the mind and transports it into other realms. It is transfiguring to simply abide on that land.

Therefore, understand well your great importance. Many of you have perceived that you are merely a *receiver* through this organization. Yet, as you receive, you are giving. And as you give, you receive. You *are* part of the Lineage, the field of energy creating a vortex that has the power to overcome illusions. Many of you are seeing this in your personal lives. Many of you are witnessing the increasing power expressed through the two who joined as one, in the physical realm, and awaited the call to join with me, and have then enacted the birthing of

Shanti Christo. And I don't think names are necessary here.

Those of you that are witnessing this increase in power through each of them, individually and collectively, you are, literally, witnessing exactly what I am talking about—that the *vortex of energy* is expanding and deepening. You are, literally, witnessing the *forerunning effects* of what is to come, when the day will arise when no one will need to say a word. And yet, through the gathering of the Lineage, individuals who are attracted will *heal* spontaneously and immediately drop into enlightenment.

All of you are part of this. This is how extraordinary you are! And this is the invitation that we constantly extend to you. Think not that that which is called Shanti Christo is simply another worldly organization. The deepest levels of transfiguration are *already occurring* through this Lineage, through this Strand or Ray of Light. Therefore, indeed, embrace that which you are, honor that which you are, extend that which you are. Go and teach all nations. Let them know that I *have* come again and that this expression, called Shanti Christo, shall become increasingly a *primary vehicle* through which the Lineage is creating the vortex, the portal, the initiation—call it what you will—the energy of transfiguration that will quicken in its Enlightenment, or Atonement, of the Sonship.

Therefore, understand well, that what will be coming in our future days and weeks, months and years together is a growing body of those maturing in the way of the Christ Mind, maturing in the level of commitment, because they will come to see the extraordinary role that they are playing in a much bigger picture than their own personal lives. The Family will, indeed, grow. And much is being set in place for this to occur. The Lineage, then, never ceases working in establishing the network of Light that allows the expression of this Light—

Lesson Ten

visibly — through this vehicle called Shanti Christo. We recognize well that, as you live your personal lives, seemingly many, many miles from one another, often with little third-dimensional contact, it is easy for the mind to cast the spell upon you that not much is occurring. And yet, I say unto you: *It will occur — with you or without you.*

The invitation, then, is to take up your rightful place by stepping into the *full commitment* for the birthing of this *extraordinary expression* that shall, indeed, eventually touch all corners of your planet. That has been its purpose since long, long, long ago. The birthing, then, of Shanti Christo is perfectly an expression of that which was just as important — called *my* birth, and my crucifixion and resurrection. *It's all part of the same script.*

Something in you has attracted you to me. Something in you has attracted you to the Lineage. Something in you *resonated* with Shanti Christo, for those words carry the vibration of the call that I have told you, from a time quite ancient, you would one day "hear" as you become "quickened from the dead" (to use a Christian phrase) — the awakening of the soul, the call back Home to the Family, to the Lineage, to the purpose of the Atonement.

Indeed, then, beloved friends, you cannot have an ordinary day any longer. You might as well accept the fact that you — let's have some fun with this here — you have come with a mission. You are a bringer of Light, a bringer of a New Day or a New Dawn. You are that which extends the Light and Love of God into Creation by your willingness to let the Light *transfigure* your humanity. Your humanity is transfigured as you *embrace* your humanity and see it *all* as *sacred*.

The Way of Knowing

For, you see, the spell of illusion is to believe that life as a body-mind is a *mistake*, that it is a fearful world, that one is limited and small, that the only thing you can do is put all your energy into trying to survive, that all you can do is block your feelings and pretend they're not there in an attempt to deny the *power* of the Christ that you are . . . the *power* to bring the miracle of Love and remembrance and Atonement to each moment.

You are, indeed, unlimited in *all ways, forever*. And the mind that serves the Holy Spirit—which *is* the Christ Mind, which *is* the Mind of Abba, which *is* the Self of your very soul; they're all the same—the mind that serves the Holy Spirit is, indeed, *unlimited forever,* and is part of an extraordinary Family, called the Lineage, that can, indeed, be traced through the Jewish nation, if you will, the Jewish families, and can be traced even back *before* that lineage, that family, that nation was birthed. It shapes itself back through Egypt, back through Persia. It has some roots in ancient India. And it, indeed, has roots beyond this physical Earth.

You, therefore, are not alone. And your role should never be minimized by you. And so, with that, please understand, that the culmination of *The Year of Knowing* has been the desire and attempt to invite you more and more and more deeply—and yes, we know that the mind hits its points of fear and must plateau out for a week or a year or ten lifetimes, before it's willing to step further. And yet, you are free, even in the midst of your deepest fears, to say, "Yes!" to transfiguration. For darkness holds no power over Light. And it is often, in fact, it is *always* when you are at the point of your greatest sense of darkness, or your greatest feeling that the Light just can't quite get into you, that you couldn't possibly ever be enlightened—it is at that moment that you need only *invite the Light.* And the Light begins to transform the darkness. It is when you are at your edge of darkness that the dawn is but a breath away.

Lesson Ten

As you transfigure *your* humanity, you are transfiguring the energy field of *humankind*, pure and simple. You are incarnating Christ into the world. You are resurrecting and awakening the "dead" into Life Eternal.

Now as we continue, then, there will, at times, be guidance from this that I am calling The Lineage. Much is going to be set in place. The quickening is going to step up a notch. And the invitation will go out to many, many more. Take up, then, your *rightful* place and begin to give up hiding your Light under a bushel. If there is anyone you know who does not yet know of your involvement in Shanti Christo, it is time to empower yourself to move beyond fear by letting them know. It is, indeed, time to start standing up to be counted as one who is committed to the transfiguration of human consciousness, through the Lineage of the Christ Mind, pure and simple.

And so, you are *extraordinarily important*. You *must* begin to discipline the mind to not perceive yourself as a small part, not to perceive yourself as separate from one another — to begin to take action to create the lines of communication, even in the third-dimensional realm. It is time for you, as individuals, to step forward in the birthing of Shanti Christo, instead of waiting and depending upon its founders or upon the handful that seem to have gone a little further ahead. You are That One you, the listener of these words. And if you will but step forward, the whole *power of the Lineage* will support you.

So, the invitation is, indeed, bold. And the "stakes," so to speak, have always been high. It is a great dream to transform the dream of separation into the Dream of Perfect Remembrance. *You are not small. And you are not alone.*

The Way of Knowing

Many of you are beginning to be more deeply aware that you, too, hear me. Let that process continue and deepen. Become an *equal conduit* which extends the Atonement, through the Christ Mind, through that which is called Shanti Christo, through you.

This, my beloved brother, was merely selected a long time ago to be the primary *initiator* of this process in space and time. That of what you might call here, the soul mate, was also part of that agreement; and yet that was only the first step. They, indeed, will continue — with you or without you. And yet, for this work to reach its fulfillment in the quickest possible time, requires the invitation of this Lineage to you, a part of this Lineage: Where can you step forward with greater boldness? Where can you find your edge of fear and call in the support of Light and move through it? Where can you drop the pebble into the pond that radiates the vibration of this Lineage through you out into the world? For the world holds no power over you.

I hope, in this simple sharing to this point, that your mind has been a little shaken, and you have been brought to a deeper stillness, that your mind has been brought back to the Reality of what attracted you to this vibration in the first place. For in that moment, your heart *was* thrown open, through the portal of initiation. Your *soul* is what has attracted you back to me, for your soul has always known the Truth, and it has simply answered the call.

Yet, it takes *vigilance* and *discipline* to always *remember* each day not to fall asleep again. For the temptation of the world is just that: to begin to think that all of those walking asleep in the world have greater knowledge than you. And since so many of them are asleep, maybe being asleep is the way to be. *It is not!* For all those sleeping will be transfigured in the twinkling of an eye. The sleeping call out in their slumber for *someone* to stir

Lesson Ten

from their sleep by *modeling* and *expressing* and *communicating* the *quickening vibration of Light* which is the presence of God.

Indeed, you have chosen to come into this dimension as part of a very grand work that is going on *multi-dimensionally*. You are, indeed, part of a rather large Family.

In the coming months and years, you will hear from me again. Many of you will continue to deepen your ability to communicate with me directly. Honor and love, therefore, one another. *Honor and love, therefore, one another.* Recognize that you've come together, not to live ordinary lives, but to play out the greatest drama ever enacted upon the human plane. That is your role, your function, your purpose, and your Life.

Understand well, then, that in the coming months, you will begin to see and witness even greater miracles and manifestations. Those of you that have been watching closely have already seen many. They will, indeed, continue to be enhanced, to be quickened. The miracles will seem bigger to some. But those of you that have been watching will know that there is no order of difficulty in miracles, and one is not greater than another. The vortex of energy is being set. Certain purifications have been occurring. And it's time for a, what you might call here, a major *pop* into another circle of energy.

You will also hear from various, what you call, members, if you will, of this Lineage that have been actively working behind the scenes, but have not stepped forward to speak. We mentioned this once before. Some of you have forgotten it. And yet, the time comes *very quickly*. You will, indeed, be hearing from That One which I have called my Mother, that you know as Mary. You will, indeed, be hearing from That One that you would know as Moses. And there will be some others as well.

The Way of Knowing

You will be hearing from what seems to be very ordinary embodied human beings, all of whom will be attracted to join with this organization because they *resonate* with the vibration that It is establishing on the planet. *Listen well* to all of them. Place no special value on communication from me or from the nonphysical realm. But listen for the strand of Truth that speaks the Reality you *know* within your heart.

It has, indeed, been a great honor to be the one selected of my Father to undergo the *laser beam purification,* called the crucifixion and resurrection, as part of a much larger picture. It has been a great honor to be the One through whom you have opened your heart to the Love of God. It has been an honor to serve as a Savior and Messiah. But in Truth, that is not the end. For *the end can come only when perfect equality as Christ is established in all hearts and minds.* Join with me, then, in this great work. *Join with me* — do not shy away from that which your heart would call you unto. Rather, *dive deeper*!

I will never leave you, and will never take my hand from this work until all is, indeed, completed. You will, indeed, be hearing from me in the future — many times. Although the vehicle through which that comes might be surprising at times.

Be you, therefore, at peace, beloved friends — beloved brothers ... and *sisters* ... who must, indeed, by the way — sisters — begin to unite more *powerfully* in the expression of the Christ Mind through the feminine form. Enough said about that for now.

I, indeed, love you always. And I participate with all minds called to awaken. I am but your brother and your friend, ever dedicated to revealing that which my Father would reveal to you through me — in just the right way, at just the right time. You are as I am. And together we transfigure humanity. In this way, then, I was a *prototype* for what is to come, an expression

Lesson Ten

in space and time of what all are destined to be. And yet, that destiny is but the *remembrance* of what they have always been, beyond the veil of illusions.

Peace is with you always. Peace is with you always. Hear the call. Accept the invitation. And let us continue in the greatest story ever told!

Amen.

The Way of Knowing

Lesson Ten Question and Answer Section

Question: There is a book out now, and it is called *The Bible Codes*. And there's been discovered a secret code in the Torah, which indicates a lot of events that have occurred now, in this time frame. Would you care to elaborate on the validity of that?

Answer: Indeed, beloved friend. It is not by accident—as nothing is—that it is come to pass that the question is being asked now. Anyone who has listened closely to what I just shared with you should have a good smile and a good laugh, recognizing that the question about these Bible codes is in perfect alignment with what has been shared.

There is, indeed, what you could call, a secret code that passes through the Torah. It will not be discovered to be as clear as expressed in the New Testament, except through *certain strands* of my teachings. That secret code is like a road map, laid *under* the field of Creation of humanity. For remember, from the time the dream of separation first entered into the mind, the Father created its *correction*. And that correction is being played out in the field of space and time. That which was called the Torah was, indeed, written by *prophets*, if you will—*mystics* would be another word; or how about *channels*?—who received guidance to tell stories, some of which, by the way, are fictional, and yet, carry what you call a mythical element. They are fiction, not as a lie, but as stories designed to prompt the soul to remember the Truth.

Within these books of the Torah, then, there has been a strand of Light, like a thread woven through it all, that carries little molecules, or little atoms of essential Truth, revealing and carrying forth God's plan for the enlightenment of His Creation. Within this strand, yes, many events have needed to come to pass. Many events in your world are secondary, or third or fourth in levels of importance. Some are quite *primary* within the greater expression of God's plan. I am mentioned in the Torah seventy times. I do not mean here by the words that you would read in your scripture of the Torah, but through that which can be revealed through these Bible codes.

All of this is to say that it was already known by the Lineage that a day would come within this Family called the Jewish nation, that a certain one would be born who is like the *fruit of the fruit*. There is some of Moses, some of Ezekiel, some of every prophet within me, as that strand of Light, emanating from Abba, *culminated* in the expression of the life of Jeshua ben Joseph, *mirroring* the Truth of every soul back to Itself, even though it was so deeply asleep. Whether it be Judas, or Esther, or Mary — all of them, every being who has ever come to hear of my Life, no matter how asleep they've been — Abba, through me, created that which models the Truth of every soul. That is what I meant when I said I was merely a prototype for what is to come, and what I meant when I said,

> *Greater works than these will you do.*

For there is great power — exponential power — when there are ten Christs as opposed to one, or fifty thousand Christs as opposed to ten. That's what's coming on your planet — *a planet of Christs*. And then, as they say in your language, *look out!*

Therefore, indeed, the code is valid. It's not by accident that it is only being unraveled now, with your high technology. It required that technology to even begin to discover it. It does, indeed, predict many events that have come to pass, but this is only to remind you that all is *already* in the Hands of your Creator. Darkness *cannot* overcome Light. Fear *cannot* defeat Love. Hell *cannot* replace Heaven. The dream of separation *cannot* replace the Reality of perfect union. The spell or illusion of what you would call *maya*, cannot come to overshadow enlightenment.

There are many ways to put that duality, but it comes down to the same thing, and it's the very same thing that I have been speaking to you for hours and hours and hours over these many years. There is something being enacted on the human plane. It is the awakening from illusion to Reality played out in the field of space and time — played out in the field of your own consciousness, which mirrors, or recapitulates, the dream that the Son of God has chosen to have. It is just a dream. And guess who wins in the end?

Yes, there is a code within the Torah. It will be found, eventually, to extend through the teachings of mine that are yet pure, and purely recorded in what is called the New Testament. But it will not be found to permeate all books of the Bible. The Torah, my teachings in the New Testament, and little smatterings here and there elsewhere.

Unfortunately, the code *requires* that the individuals using it be willing to ask *bold* questions. So far, they have asked conservative questions because they are conservatively-minded. But that's perfectly okay. All that matters here is that you recognize that this is simply more evidence for the Truth I have shared with you many times. Namely, that in the moment the dream of separation was created, the Father created the correction, and it is in place. It's already occurring, it's always been occurring, and *it will not fail*!

Does that sufficiently answer your request?

Q: Yes. Can you explain more about the free will of children, because it often appears that they are at the mercy of their

Lesson Ten

parents' choices?

A: Remember that in the bigger picture there is only One Mind, playing out the dream of separation and awakening to the Reality of Love. Now, in the complexity of this journey there is that which is called "karma," would be your word. There is that which is the truth that the sins of the fathers are visited unto the third and fourth generation. That is, the *energetic patterns of perception* are handed, one mind to another, until some mind begins to awaken. When you are asleep, and lost in darkness, you will take hold of any hand extended to you. Why? Because your desire is to survive.

The desire, by the way, to survive in the physical form is but an analog, or an expression, or a metaphor, for the *soul's desire to survive in God*, to awaken to the Truth of the Christ. I've said to you many times that everything is just a symbol for the spiritual journey. So therefore, when you look upon your children, all the children of this planet, *of course* there is a stage in which they seem to be influenced by the psychic field of the parents, peers, teachers. This recapitulates the fall into the dream of separation and the choice of every soul to awaken. But awakening requires the embrace of humanity's shadow side, or darkness. You cannot embrace what you do not first own as a part of you. Therefore, the soul takes *on* the shadow, takes *on* the cloak of the dream of separation, and then *decides* whether it will be a *victim* of that, or whether it will be transfigured *in spite of it*, and, therefore, overcome the world.

Each soul, in its particular expression, has its own unique dynamics, in terms of how it has fallen under the spell, and how it is choosing to go about requiring or learning the lessons it desires in its way of releasing, bit by bit, fear of the extraordinary Truth of its being.

So, from one perspective, it looks like a child is a poor victim. That is part of the game of separation being played out. In Reality, it is not possible to be a victim. *It is not possible to be a victim.* Nothing can come unless it is called.

The experience of every child is by the sovereign power of that soul. And the lessons that it is garnering are rich and varied. This is why you cannot compare anyone's journey. What you can do is *honor* everyone's journey. Never look upon another and say,

> *I'm so sorry you've had that experience.*

Rather, learn to ask of them,

> *What has this taught you? How will you choose to respond to this condition? Will you choose victimhood, or will you choose transfiguration?*

Which is to say,

> *Will you accept the power within you to heal, or will you require, through lack of forgiveness, the continuation of your belief that you are small, that you are unworthy. Which would you choose to create?*

I'm not saying do not be compassionate. Quite to the contrary, *passion* means to *enter into passion with*. Compassion, community—to join with, in passion. But empathy should never be sympathy.

Trust, then, your children and the path that they choose. Indeed, learn to love them as an aspect of your own soul. And yet, give them complete freedom to choose. It is extremely important. The sovereignty of the soul is sacred above all Creation.

Lesson Ten

Does that help you in regard to your question?

Response: Yes.

Jeshua: You see, often when an adult looks upon the plight of a child, and *feels* helpless, or *feels* that this is wrong, or *feels anger*, all they are doing is expressing a tender point that has not been healed within *themselves* regarding their own childhood experiences. It is an *edge* being revealed to *them* that calls for deeper healing and forgiveness in *themselves*. For only those that can forgive themselves, only those that have healed within themselves, can, indeed, be of any value in helping another to heal.

I once said unto you that those who speak and work for peace, but do not have peace in their own hearts, accomplish nothing. It is no different than working with a child who's been abused, who's been hungry, who's going through turmoil with peers, whatever it is. If it is activating *your emotion*, look well to see what might yet remain unhealed within *yourself*. In other words, take the log out of your own eye, before you attempt to help another with the speck of dust in their own — that looks like a log because you are projecting what is unhealed within yourself. Only the *healed mind* can assist in the healing of another.

We'll let that answer, then, be sufficient for now.

Response: Thank you.

Jeshua: Indeed, you are most welcome.

And unto all of you then, again, blessings and peace be with you always.

The Way of Knowing

PERSONAL NOTES

Lesson Ten

PERSONAL NOTES

The Way of Knowing

PERSONAL NOTES

Lesson Eleven

Lesson Eleven

Now, we begin.

And once again, greetings unto you, beloved and holy friends. Again, I come forth to abide with you because I love you. Always, then, and forever we are joined in the place of Love. Always and forever we are joined in the place of Reality. Always and forever I am but your brother and your friend. You have many brothers, and many sisters, in what you call the disembodied state, who know you and who love you and who do not come closer to you than you are willing to allow. And that allowance is always the result of your decision to claim your *worthiness* to have communication that can enlighten you.

You are then, indeed, entirely sovereign at all times. You, and you alone, create the thoughts, the beliefs, the perceptions, that you wish to experience. These then crystallize into the forms of your experience, even into the physical dimension. Remember then, in this conclusion of this year's *Way of Knowing*, that there is never a time that you see anything that exists outside of you. Everything you see originates within you, since the only thing you *can* see is the way in which *you* choose to cloak or drape the mysterious energy of Creation.

Every neutral event, every moment of arising, is merely energy given to you on a silver platter, if you will — given to you freely that you, as consciousness, might choose to have the opportunity *to create experience* by *cloaking that energy*, that has been presented to you, with the perceptions and beliefs that you have *chosen* for yourself. You have heard me say unto you many times that only Love is Real. You have heard me say unto you many times that it is not necessary to seek for Love, but it *is* necessary to seek for what is false.

In these past three years, you have been given many, many tools and much deep and profound understanding to assist you into the simple decision of complete responsibility for every moment of your experience. For in the end, I can give you only this. I cannot *relieve* you of what you may perceive yet to be the *burden* of the fact that you *are constantly creating*—that you are, indeed, a Creator.

Likewise, I would not wish to unburden you from the incredible, shimmering awareness and responsibility—the freedom, the fun of knowing that as a *sovereign master* of your domain, you are free to create whatever your heart most truly desires.

The secret then, as I have shared with you many times, is to *practice seeking first the Kingdom*. Never let a day go by in which you fail to ponder the great mystery of God's Presence. Never let a morning go by that you fail to begin your day, except in this way: surrender all thought of what you know and have believed. Rest in gratitude to the One Who has birthed you. Ask only to be revealed for you greater Truth, greater wisdom, greater capacity to know and extend perfect Love, perfect trust and perfect peace.

In *The Way of Knowing* we come to the great culmination that you are, indeed, as I Am. That in each moment of your soul's journey, you have, literally, created the worlds of your experience—just as I did when I walked upon your plane, just as I continue to do now. How, then, has it occurred that this form of communication could take place? It is not so much that I cleverly set up a labyrinth of doorways to draw this, my beloved brother, into a place in which I could connect with him. But rather, I rested in my desire to extend the Atonement.

By creating that desire, I began to create a vibrational field emanating from my mind out through Creation. That vibration, alone, is not enough. But where it resonated with the deepest

Lesson Eleven

(and, at that time, fairly well hidden) desire of this, my beloved brother, to know the Christ Mind, to find a way to serve, to indeed heal and awaken from any last traces of illusion — it is like two wires dancing about, their dance caused by the movement of energy through them, until their energy touches, joining the tips of the wires together. That is when the flow began. That is when I could appear to him in his living room.

The same process must have occurred between my mind and yours, or you would not be listening to this tape. You would have never heard of Shanti Christo. And you would not have heard of me. Recognize, then, *your own power*. For you have attracted me unto yourself, as I have attracted you to me. And in each moment of all of your relationships, whether they be with people, places or things, learn to pause long enough (which only takes a few seconds) and say within yourself,

> *I am in the moment of this relationship because I have called this to myself. There is, then, something within me which vibrates or resonates perfectly with the "other."*

Again, whether that be person, place, or thing.

True change, then, can occur, not when you recognize that you don't like the relationship you're in, of person, place or thing, and therefore take steps to get yourself out of it — but rather, when you recognize that the relationship and what is occurring within it must be the result of something within your own consciousness. And, therefore, what is unlikable in that moment of relationship is merely the flowering of a *seed potential*, or vibration, that you have been holding in the depth of your own being. It is, then, a simple thing to seek first the Kingdom, to rest in that simple knowingness, and to gently inquire of the Holy Spirit to teach you, to reveal to you, what you have held as a true belief that is, indeed, false as you then see why you have been holding that belief, and how it has manifested the world of your experience, you then are quite free to choose anew.

It is just at this point where so often the mind becomes fearful,

But at least I know *this. I do not know what is unknown.*

But I say unto you, there is nothing *un*known. There is *nothing* unknown to you. For there *is* nothing until *you* decide to *choose* for it. This is why *desire* is the first key to the Kingdom. Freedom can only come to the mind that truly assumes complete responsibility for the creation of its experience. So that in any moment, it recognizes that the thoughts, the perceptions, and the feelings coursing through the emotional body are arising within the sovereign domain of that soul's being. They are *uncaused* save, again, for the seed thoughts or perceptions that that mind, or that soul, has chosen to value for itself.

Life, then, offers you your way out. When things don't seem to be working and your "piece" is missing, this is actually a sign to you that there must be some belief or perception that you are clinging to which does not work. You are free, then, to seek it out, to inquire, and then to change it.

I have often recommended to you that you cannot transcend what you first fail to embrace. Therefore, look well upon your creations—and bless them. If it is the fact that your car has just broken down along the freeway, and the wheels have fallen off, and the motor's stopped, and the doors have crumbled to dust—bless it. For that context of experience will take you into your tomorrows.

Lesson Eleven

There is no moment, then, and this is the point that we're reaching, *there is no moment*, in which you have *failed*. As a sovereign master, indeed, the literal embodiment of the Mind of God, you have used your freedom to create experience. Embrace it. Rest in gratitude for it. Own it as completely yours. And then simply ask,

Do I wish to continue it, or would I like to start a new adventure?

You will be creating new adventures eternally. For there is no moment that Creation ends. And *mind*, or *soul*, is the *vortex*, the *vehicle* through which Creation extends Itself from the field of infinite possibility into the realization of manifold particularities.

Beloved friends, you are, indeed, as I Am. I'm rather enjoying my domain. I am unlimited by space and time, and have no longer any need, whatsoever, for the unique forms of experience that can come through the crystallization of what you call the body—what some of you still mistakenly call *yourself*.

You, then, are very much at play in the Kingdom, like a child in a sandbox. And each event that arises for you need not be judged. I have shared with you many times that it is the egoic mind that compares and contrasts. Therefore, *never* compare or contrast your experience with another person's. Yours is unique. And though the world would say, perhaps, that your experience isn't as valuable because you are only worth twenty thousand dollars and somebody else is worth four hundred million, therefore they have manifested more powerfully—that is simply not true. For manifestation is simply the expression that reveals where the mind has been focusing.

The Way of Knowing

The *real* power is the very mystery that *anything* can be manifested *at all*. And you are free to constantly choose anew. Cultivate, then, a very childlike attitude toward *all* of your experience. Learn to ponder it, to wonder about it, to look upon it like a father does to a child, like your Father does to you.

Behold, I have created all things and it is good!

In your Bible, in the creation story that is told there, it is said that God said something like that. For God looked upon all that He had created and said,

Behold, it is very good!

You are the father of your creations. You are the father of your thoughts, your attitudes, and your choices. Look upon all of these things and say,

Behold, it is very good.

For goodness begets goodness. Judgment begets judgment. For nothing can produce except that which is like itself. An acorn cannot produce a fish. A man and a woman cannot produce an acorn. The thoughts you hold about yourself will reproduce themselves. When you look upon all things as good, goodness will be begotten from that decision.

Each time, then, that you have chosen to hold a negative thought about yourself, or about anyone, you have only ensured the kind of inconsistency in your mind that interrupts the power of your ability to create, more and more, as a living embodied master. This can only be because you have held deep within the mind some belief that says,

No *matter what I do, it won't work out.*

Lesson Eleven

There is some *conflicted* belief. A belief in goodness and a belief in evil create a conflict that must entrap the soul.

Therefore, indeed, beloved friends, if you are to complete this year of *The Way of Knowing*, then know this: As you think, so shall you be. And how you think, how you choose to perceive and believe, will determine what you see in the world. And what you believe you see will determine how you act. It will determine the friends you keep, the kind of career you create, where you live, and how you feel.

In other words, if you hold the thought that you cannot trust the Universe to support you, you will look out and see a world that seems, self-evidently, to reveal to you that such a thought is true. You will then create behaviors to insulate yourself and never let the world know what you want. And then, of course, you will wonder why life seems to go on as it always has.

Learn, then, always to inquire, not out into the world but into yourself:

> *If I am having this experience, what must I have believed to be true about myself and about the world?*

The truth will come, through prayer and through honesty. And when you discover it, you will know it. And then use the sovereign power of free choice given unto you, which is, indeed, the Truth of the Kingdom, to choose otherwise.

A master cannot *blame*. And a master can never perceive him or herself as having been victimized. And yet, this mastery doesn't come through special spiritual power. It comes only through a simple and free choice. Remember, I said earlier that you are constantly creating your experience. You are free in this moment, and in every moment, to simply say,

I believe I'll adopt the perspective of a master — no sense in blame, no sense in feeling like a victim. What I'm experiencing is wholly mine. I must, therefore, have wanted it.

Always be very careful, then, that you do not judge what is occurring. For that is the fault that people fall into.

Why did I call this to myself? This is a horrible experience. Why, oh why, did I want this?

All of that is judgment and not gratitude. I learned at the crucifixion that I could feel and experience gratitude for my persecutors. I could feel gratitude for the whole context of experience that *I had chosen to call to myself* in order to discover that there are *no* circumstances powerful enough to prevent me from choosing for Love.

And in the end, can there be a more powerful experience to call to yourself than that? (laughing) Not the crucifixion, with nails in your wrists but, rather, the power to see that in every moment — of birth and of death, of comings and goings — that nothing prevents you from the deep peace and joy of choosing to Love. For Love is not conditioned by the conditions of the world. How can it be, when the world does not exist? Only you exist, as a field of awareness that chooses to create perception and belief.

Beloved friends, the world *is* unreal. In the end, the body is unreal, at least as you perceive it to be, for the body cannot limit you in any way. You already extend so far beyond it that it seems unimaginable and completely unbelievable. You are, indeed, the Thought of Love in form. But that form is not the body. It is merely the Thought or the Reality which is Christ. Christ is the essence of your higher Self. Christ is the Truth of Who you Are. And the role of the body, then, can only be to

Lesson Eleven

bless, to comfort, and to extend Love.

Two lovers find the fulfillment of their lovemaking, in your physical plane, when each delights only in blessing, comforting, and extending Love. Each learns, yes, to receive that desire from the other, as an act of Love toward that one.

> *Oh, let me massage your shoulders.*
>
> *Okay!*

For relationship *is* the means of your salvation. And holy relationship is always a simple, joyful dance of two who recognize, truly, that only Love is Real and they want nothing else.

You are, indeed, a sovereign master of your domain. You cannot fail at any moment. And any form of experience that is unfolding for you is merely the fruit of the seeds of thought that you have planted within your mind. Look at the outcome in order to discover the thought. And then merely ask, by first saying,

> *What a good girl am I (or a good boy am I). That was a rich experience. Hmm, I wonder what I might most want to experience now?*

For rest assured you *will* experience it.

You can, then, either claim dominion over your life, and become the conscious director of your life experience, or you can abdicate it to someone else— such as your government, your employer, or what have you. You are totally free to do that if you remember to claim it as a sovereign act.

The Way of Knowing

> *I am commuting two hours on this freeway to a job that I don't like, and commuting home for two hours every day. Because of the sovereignty of my total mastery, I choose to do so.*

For that is the only reason you can find yourself in any place at any time.

As a sovereign master, you are free to follow me. You are free to *choose only* your loving thoughts. You are free to *remember only* your loving thoughts. You are free to embrace whatever comes up that may be unlike Love and simply accept that it must be an old seed getting cooked, and that you are free to embrace *it* with Love. This is why there can be no *feeling* that must be judged or avoided. Feelings of despair, or feelings of sadness — these things are merely something left over from a past thought. And in the act of embracing them, you have already decided with Love. And Love, alone, heals all things.

And so, just think of this. As a sovereign master you chose, without lifting a finger, to call into the domain of your experience a form of communication with an ancient friend — Jeshua ben Joseph. Out of the field of your sovereign domain as a living master, you have chosen that called Shanti Christo into your domain. There *must* be a reason for it. There must be a desire for it. And is that not the desire to discover, ever more deeply, if there is anything possibly obstructing you from experiencing greater joy, greater peace, greater wisdom, and greater Christed Consciousness?

For, indeed, beloved friends, a master never ceases in growing him or herself. A master is never finished. Do not think that you can come to the end of some form of experience, perhaps even the death of the body-mind, and suddenly be at the finish line. For there is no such thing as a finish line. There are only realms that you can grow into in which Creation is indeed far more

Lesson Eleven

blissful than it is in the physical domain. But Creation continues. Your responsibility and your sovereignty and your dominion continue.

For the further you go into God, the greater the responsibility, for you are dealing with greater power. Thus the need for vigilance and discipline does not go away; it *increases*, but a master *welcomes* it. For through it even greater creations can flow through their holy mind. Did you know that it is possible to birth an entire, what you might call, a solar system with a single thought?

Now, if you've ever baked a very good chocolate cake, you know something of what it means to create. If you've ever written a poem, if you've ever birthed a child, if you've ever planted a seed and watched it grow, then you know and understand the great satisfaction of creating. Imagine merely holding a thought in the mind and then experiencing the actual birthing of an entire solar system. It is, indeed, a great delight!

Imagine birthing something like Shanti Christo by merely emanating a vibration that is resonant with the desire of this, my beloved brother's mind, for instance, and that of the "twin." Imagine birthing that which is called *A Course in Miracles* merely by holding the thought of it in its completed form, and then letting that wave emanate and join with another mind, who happens to be in the physical domain and does all the work.

That is the power that is available to you. And as you choose to embrace yourself as a master, as you choose to look upon each and every moment of your experience as wholly self-created, as that which is waiting for *your* blessing, as you come to see that there is power and freedom in choosing to bless with gratitude *all* of your creation and then to say,

The Way of Knowing

This has been so fantastic. It might be fun to have something even greater happen now! It was great being with that lover, but what the heck, they've just recently died, so I think I'll open up to something even greater.

It is that kind of an attitude that expands the Kingdom, the domain of your consciousness, until the day arises when the physical universe can no longer contain you. And you will simply outshine the body itself.

This has occurred, by the way. Some minds have outshined the body before the body was ready to die. They merely dissolved in Light and that was the end of it. It is not necessary, however, to do so. For the experience of what is called "death" in your world is *just another experience*. If you bring your awareness to it, you will discover in the day of what you call death that it's actually rather delightful. As your attention withdraws from the body, you become the witness of the gasping of the lungs, the building up of the fluid, and you watch it with disinterest. For you are already vibrating in the energy of bliss, which *is* the essence of your soul. Death, then, is quite simply, nothing.

Beloved friends, in the culmination, then, of this year of *The Way of Knowing*, I ask you as your equal, and as your brother, and as your friend eternally, to claim in this hour *complete sovereign mastery* over your domain. Discover what has not yet been embraced and owned. For those things which are dissociated, in your psychological language, that which has not been *embraced* by you, *imprisons* you. There is the doorway to perfect freedom. There the doorway into what looks like the unknown, except that there is no such thing as the unknown. For nothing exists until you call it to yourself.

In this year, then, of *The Way of Knowing*, let its culmination be that as this tape ends and you click off your button, let it be the

Lesson Eleven

last act you ever do with a mind that says,

> *I'm still trying to get there. I'm still a victim of the world I see.*

When you click it off, let those attitudes be clicked off entirely. It requires only the willingness to say in each moment,

> *This must be what I have called to myself. Do I wish to continue it, or would I choose something else?*

The world, then, you have made is only an illusion. Nothing which has been constructed must remain *unless you desire it*. If you continue the structures of your life—career, relationship, whatever it is—recognize that you are doing so out of the sheer delight of wanting the experience. And if you prefer, you can let it crumble and start anew. You are free to clear out your bank accounts, give away all of your material possessions, sign over your house to somebody else, give your car keys to somebody and simply start walking down the road with nothing but the clothing on your back. You are totally free to do that. And out of the power of your desire, you will attract situations that provide a place to sleep, food to eat, new experiences and new friends.

At no time can *anyone* be a victim. And yet at any time, consciousness is free to perceive itself as *having been* victimized. That is merely the choice to create a form of experience. We might share with you that victimization is one of the "booby prizes" chosen pervasively by humanity: the victim game. Many are quite committed to seeing how well they can play it out. One could say that the victimization game has affected virtually every mind in the human domain.

You are not a victim. If, indeed, tomorrow, your doctor tells you,

263

The Way of Knowing

> *You have cancer and you have fifteen days left to live. I wish you would have come in earlier. I could have given you, possibly, forty-five days.*

Simply say to yourself,

> *Oh, what a rich experience this might be. I have fifteen days to go into the death of the body with total consciousness, complete forgiveness, and perfect peace. Wow, what an amazing opportunity I have called to myself!*

For cancer is not a failure. Indeed, we would behold, in much of your so-called New Age movement, that there is much judgment — *much judgment* — much abhorrence of anything that doesn't look like manifesting wealth, having the perfectly curved hips, and a multitude of loving friends. That is a naive attitude.

But the soul's sovereignty is rich beyond measure. *Wherever you are as you listen to these words, you are living sovereign mastery, now.* And you are free to create anew any time you wish. But understand that the experience you are having, when embraced and loved and accepted totally as being uncaused by anything but your own awareness, when you can *delight in that*, you are free — you are free! And you have already risen above and gone far beyond the most successful beings that *humanity* would say are successful.

Do not, then, be succumbed to the shimmering lights of the world, the great tinsel on the tree. For all that matters is this:

> *Am I at peace? Do I bring Love to each moment? Do I accept (laughing) with great humor, that all that I have experienced has been by my own design, an interesting game, and perhaps a joke, played upon myself?*

Lesson Eleven

To look upon the world and say,

There is nothing I need here. But I choose to be here to see who I can love, how I can love, and what enjoyment I might create.

Peace, then, is always the goal of the spiritual journey—that Peace that passes all understanding. For if you have listened well to what I have shared with you in this hour, ninety-five percent of it seems like mere gibberish to the world:

It cannot be that way!

It turns the world upside down, rips it inside out and makes it *valueless*. But it makes *you* valuable. It places you at the right hand of God. This is what you were birthed for. This is where you remain. For Love waits on your welcome.

And so I greet you, indeed, beloved friends, as my equal. I greet you as sovereign masters, co-creators, perfect divine expressions of creativity, ceaselessly creating all that you would choose to experience. I never lament the pain that you experience. I never feel sorry for your suffering. I merely wait, in Love, for the Truth of your being, and offer assistance to you, when you are willing to grow, to heal, to forgive, to expand, and to enlighten your being.

Great freedom can come when, in the midst of something that you feel to be great suffering, you choose to laugh and say,

Look at this one! What an amazing script I have written here. I ought to win – what is that called in your world? – the Oscar-winning play here. Who could have done this one better than this?

And rest assured, you are speaking to one who had some experience at writing rather interesting scripts of suffering.

The Way of Knowing

Beloved friends, look *lovingly* upon the world you have created. Look with perfect forgiveness *now* upon the simplicity of your physical domain. For the life of the body- mind arises and passes away in a few cosmic seconds. You can delight in sensory experience, indeed in the "cruel beauty of time," without ever believing that it should be different than it is. It is merely shadow. It is merely a disguise that you have laid upon a mysterious energy. For you, indeed, have birthed the physical domain, itself. You might as well *relax and enjoy it.*

In each and every one of your days, then, live and behave as a master lives and behaves. When first you realize that you are awake in the physical domain in the morning, choose Love. Choose to relax the body-mind into a state of deep prayer and give thanks to your Creator. Hold in the mind's eye all of your domain—your relationships, your careers, your physical objects and say,

> *Behold* [laughing], *it's been a gas!*

Then simply ask,

> *I wonder if there is anything I might like to move toward changing in order to experience greater joy, deeper peace, more certain wisdom, and more loving relationship?*

If something comes into your mind, do not blame it, do not judge it, but simply begin to *wonder* about how you might like to see it changed. Hold that as a desire in the depth of your consciousness. And if its energy builds during the course of the day, simply begin to say it, write it out, get a picture of it, hold the desire in your heart. And you will, indeed, bring it to pass. For you see, manifestation occurs *instantaneously* in the field of a mind that is no longer conflicted with opposite kinds of thoughts.

Lesson Eleven

So if anything seems to be manifesting slowly for you, first of all it simply may be that that's part of your script. That's the journey you are taking. A walk from one village to the next allows a much richer experience than taking a taxi. It may also be because you have some conflicted belief in your mind, and therefore in the cells of your body, that is not in alignment with what you would wish to desire. For instance, often the human mind will say,

I desire a perfect loving relationship.

But deep in the quiet of the mind is the thought,

Except I don't deserve it. I'm unlovable.

When that has been repressed or dissociated, it will run you and will conflict, or take away from you, the power to create or to attract the desire. Therefore, when you desire, look well and watch with subtle vigilance, what *contrary thoughts* seem to also come up in the mind. Then follow those contrary thoughts so that they become crystal clear. You may even discover where they began. Feel whatever feelings may be associated with them, yes, and then return to what you desire until you feel that all of your being is in perfect alignment with it. For then you begin to create yourself as a resonating station to which those things will be called that help align your external world in the physical domain to *express* the desire you've created.

One who, for instance, creates a life-style of financial independence after twenty or thirty years, from one perspective has accomplished a great deal, but from another has taken a very long, slow way to get there. Everyone is free to create what they desire. Everyone is free to do so because they are doing it, now. Look well, then, to the feeling and the thought coursing through you. Look well to the physical environment in which you find yourself. Look well to the objects that you have surrounded yourself with and simply say,

> *All of these things demonstrate to me what I have chosen to desire. And it is very good!*

That statement of Love and acceptance is the doorway to expansion of your mastery. For in Truth, as the master awakens to what they have been doing all along, the most natural thing in the world is to create greater joy.

And the highest level of joy is to manifest service to the Atonement. That is why, perhaps one gives up a job in a corporation to go and start to make videos that can help get a good message out to the world. That is why someone ceases to work in a doctor's office and becomes a channel for Jeshua. That is why someone drops what they are doing in a corporate career and becomes a minister — because within them the soul has said,

> *Okay, enough of that experience. I want greater joy. And the pathway to greater joy is to join with like minds that are creating and extending contexts in which other minds can awaken.*

That is why many of you have been attracted to Shanti Christo, to join with, to use your golden coins, to use your voice, to use your lips, to use your hands, to use your feet, to help participate in the creation of contexts in which the Atonement can occur.

Service, then, is the natural outflow of a heart filled with the gratitude of Grace. Masters are never found struggling to survive in something they don't like. They would frankly rather sit on a street corner, asking passers-by for a nickel or two to get a cup of coffee. Meanwhile they're too busy smiling and waving and blessing everyone that walks by because they

Lesson Eleven

would rather love than look good in the world. A master has no choice but to serve — but to serve not from *duty*, but from *joy*. For the greatest joy can be to extend the *good*, the *holy*, and the *beautiful*.

Therefore, when you choose active participation in serving the Atonement, you will discover that you will, indeed, be well supported. And all of the events that occur are merely opportunities to deepen your capacity for wisdom, for peace, and for Love — to create within yourself a conduit for the extension of greater Love into the world — not because you *must*, but because you've *chosen* to serve. And you've chosen to serve because it is the greatest source of joy. If, then, you resist service, it must mean that there is some seed thought within you that is in conflict with the desire to serve, and that is all.

And so, indeed, beloved friends, we come, then, very gently, and by way of summation, to the culmination of this year of *The Way of Knowing*. The Truth is, you've been a master all along. You cannot help but be one, for you are constantly creating your experience. You are free now to create *differently*. How to do that? Do not get up out of your chair and rush about. But why not decide, right now, to experience happiness, to experience peace, and to experience the knowledge that you *are* a master.

How do you do that? By *choosing* to. Simply decide right now for the next thirty seconds to be happy. And then choose another thirty seconds to be at peace, and then another thirty seconds to simply and quietly look around you and say,

> *Behold, I am, indeed, the master of my domain. And all of it has been very, very good.*

Thank the chair that you are sitting in for coming into your domain. Thank the vase of flowers on your table. Thank the electricity bill that comes in the mail. Thank *all* things as blessings that come to you.

For to fail to do this contracts your power to continue to expand and to create what you enjoy. To *believe* that you are in lack at any time is to *create* lack in your tomorrows. Therefore, choose now to *feel* perfect abundance and joy. And then *behave* as one who *knows* they live in abundance.

I love you. You love me. This communication will never cease. And why? Because I have no intention of withdrawing myself from extending the Christ Mind to anyone who will receive it.

We are, indeed, joined in the place of Perfect Love. Creation is merely a harmless game, done for the simple enjoyment of creating. Become, then again, as a little child, for every master *is* a little child, delighting in the great mystery and the seeming surprises of discovering the power that can move through them.

Always move toward what you enjoy. Always follow your heart.

Do not follow the reactive ego that says,

Oh, no. I don't want to go there because that feels uncomfortable.

Nothing is uncomfortable. It's just another opportunity to have an experience to broaden your capacity to love. How can I say that? Try the crucifixion. It was not uncomfortable, once I embraced it. This is why, by the way, and some of you have done this, why human beings can walk on fire and not burn their feet. Why? Because they choose to do so and have a good experience. And everything in them is unconflicted for at least the minute or so it takes to do the firewalk. That gives them a

Lesson Eleven

taste of what is possible *always*.

Use, then, your time to cultivate the garden of a Healed Mind. Never believe that you do not hold the power to change the energy you feel in your emotional body, to change the thoughts held within the mind. You are free to birth whatever you so desire. And nothing can serve as a limit to *you*.

Peace, then, be with you this day! Peace, then, be with you always.

We are, indeed, looking forward to your coming year in which there will be others to communicate with you, as well, as we will seek to *magnetize*, to *direct*, to *suggest* that other minds—with bodies and without—come to bring you messages of Truth and of wisdom and of skills that can help you perfect your mastery in the world.

You are free. You are Home. You are, as I am.

Peace, then, be unto you always, precious, precious friends.

Amen.

The Way of Knowing

PERSONAL NOTES

Lesson Eleven

PERSONAL NOTES

PERSONAL NOTES

Lesson Eleven

WayofMasteryBooks.com
Book Catalog

All New releases will be announced on the website as well as access to Kindle/ eReader versions and special audio offerings

IN BOOKSTORES

The Way of Heart
The Christ Mind Trilogy
Volume I

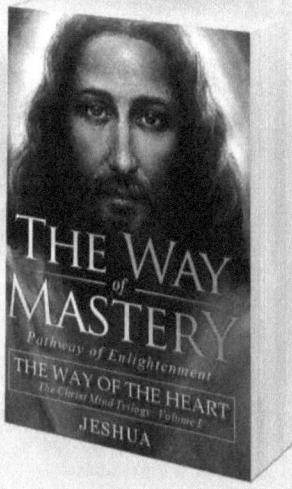

The Way of the Heart is the first of The Christ Mind Trilogy teachings, the core, formal, lessons of The Way of Mastery Pathway.

The lessons here are ones that Jeshua Himself was given in His lifetime, and subjects include the nature and meaning of reality, the power of forgiveness, purified desire as alignment to the Will of God, the four "Keys to the Kingdom," and much more.

The Way of the Heart teachings and experiential learnings provides the firm and essential foundation for all of that which follows in The Christ Mind Trilogy. It is a key aspect of Jeshua's Pathway of Enlightenment, and His Promise to us to help us awaken from the illusion that we have ever been separate from God, and to remember the deepest Truth of who we are: Christ.

ISBN 978-1-941489-41-3
Available in Paperback, Hardcover, Kindle, eReader & Audiobook

IN BOOKSTORES

The Way *of* Transformation
The Christ Mind Trilogy
Volume II

The *Way of Transformation* is the second of The *Christ Mind Trilogy* teachings, or the 'Way of' Lessons. These were originally recorded as live channelings of Jeshua, and later transcribed. Together, the trilogy forms an in-depth three year Course in *The Way of Mastery* devoted to healing the illusions that bind us beyond mere 're-training' of the mind. It is meant to be read and studied only after the student has completed *The Way of the Heart* text and lessons.

Hear what Jeshua says of it:

"The Way of Transformation absolutely requires that you be committed to living differently. For is not transformation a change from the status quo? How can you experience transformation if you do not use time to think and be differently? Crying out to me will not do it. Reading a thousand holy books will not do it. One thing, and one thing only, will bring you into the transformation that you have sought — the willingness to abide where you are, differently."

The Way of Transformation teachings and experiential learnings provide the firm and critical foundation for *The Way of Knowing*, the final part of *The Christ Mind Trilogy*.

ISBN 978-1-941489-42-0
Available in Paperback, Hardcover, Kindle, eReader & Audiobook

IN BOOKSTORES

The Way *of* Knowing
The Christ Mind Trilogy
Volume III

The *Way of Knowing* is the third and final teaching of *The Christ Mind Trilogy*, a Course originally recorded as live channelings of Jeshua over a three year period, and foundational to the larger Way of Mastery Pathway. It is meant to be read and studied only after the student has completed *The Way of the Heart* and *The Way of Transformation* texts and lessons. In Jeshua's own words:

"In *The Way of Knowing*, the *final surrender* is entered — that surrender which is beyond the comprehension of all the languages and theologies of your world, beyond all that can be spoken or uttered, yet not what can be *known, felt, realized, and lived!*"

Here, He unequivocally tells us that what we consider as 'knowledge' is a pale substitute for the mystical transfiguration the Christ Path is truly devoted to:

"Knowledge is a knowing by being that which is known."

Following the completion of the *Christ Mind Trilogy*, Jeshua begins the astounding restoration of His original Aramaic Teachings, notably the Lords Prayer and Beatitudes, along with a one year online Course for the maturing student called *Jewels of the Christ Mind*.

ISBN 978-1-941489-43-7
Available in Paperback, Hardcover, Kindle, eReader & Audiobook

IN BOOKSTORES

The Jeshua Letters
A Remarkable Encounter with Christ

In July 1987, Jesus (Jeshua) appeared out of a field of light, fully formed, to his chosen channel and scribe Jayem. Over a period of nearly two years Jeshua appeared many times and gave 'dictation', which Jayem recorded, and which became the earliest parts of *The Way of Mastery Pathway*. Eventually Jeshua asked that these be published, and they, along with Jayem's personal reflections on how all this unfolded, make up *The Jeshua Letters*.

The Jeshua Letters is the start of an astounding body of work given by Jeshua which restore the essential truths of His original teachings, previously 'lost in translation' in their passage from Aramaic to English. Jeshua's 'Letters' are simple, profound and practical. His voice is certain but always gentle; inviting, never demanding. To read them is know beyond doubt - to know palpably - that Truth is being expressed.

ISBN 978-1-941489-45-1 • *Available in Paperback, Hardcover, Kindle, eReader*

IN BOOKSTORES

The Way *of the* Servant

The Way of the Servant is the second text dictated by Jeshua and scribed by Jayem in *The Way of Mastery Pathway*, following The Jeshua Letters.

Jeshua oftens speaks of "beginning at the end", and here He does so, showing us nothing less than how the Pathway flowers as the highest pinnacle of Consciousness (fully realized Christ Mind) that can be known in this world: *true servantship*, devoted to the realization of Humanity's highest evolution or, the 'coming of heaven to earth'.

Short, succinct, of extraordinary mystical depth, countless Pathway students find that immersing in *Way of the Servant* every year reveals depths and brings illuminations they were incapable of truly comprehending before!

ISBN 978-1-941489-44-4 • *Available in Paperback, Hardcover, Kindle, eReader*

IN BOOKSTORES

The Early Years
Volume I
Now, We Begin

The Early Years (volumes I & II) are transcriptions of gatherings recorded live as Jeshua taught us all. The wisdom, guidance, and sheer brilliance of them is astounding; there is so much in these pages, dear reader, that will help you grow in understanding, support you to truly heal into peace, and more!

Volume one includes the talks below:
- Awakening
- Choose to See
- Death Earth Changes
- Decide to be Christ
- Grace as Reality
- Healing
- Heaven on Earth
- Ignorance is Bliss
- Joy I
- Joy II

ISBN 978-1-941489-46-8 • *Available in Paperback, Hardcover, Kindle, eReader*

IN BOOKSTORES

The Early Years
Volume II
Now, We Begin

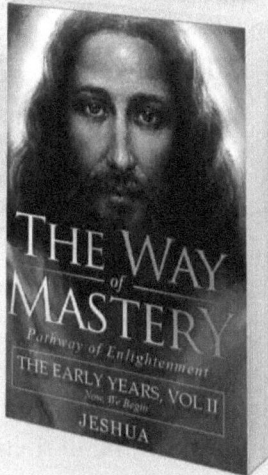

The Early Years (volumes I & II) are transcriptions of gatherings recorded live as Jeshua taught us all. The wisdom, guidance, and sheer brilliance of them is astounding; there is so much in these pages, dear reader, that will help you grow in understanding, support you to truly heal into peace, and more!

Volume two includes the talks below:
- Mastering Communication
- The Blessing of Forgiveness
- The Divine Feminine
- The Holy Instant
- The Holy Spirit
- The Light that You are
- Walk with Me
- Love Heals All Things
- The Meaning of Ascension
- Teach Only Love
- The Heart of Freedom
- The Master of Time

ISBN 978-1-941489-47-5 • *Available in Paperback, Hardcover, Kindle, eReader*

COMING SOON

Darshan

Over a period of 3 years, originally in live group video recordings, Jayem offered for the first time an in depth immersion into each lesson of The Way of Mastery Christ Mind Trilogy. He reveals the rich beauty and practical wisdom of the Teachings and shares transforming insights into their timeless Lessons, garnered from his own studentship of them for over some 25 years.

This is a remarkable and vast treasure trove of material, and we anticipate 6-8 volumes as we transcribe over 178 hours of audio into written form.

COMING SOON

The Later Years

While Jeshua guided Jayem deeply into the Aramaic Teachings and their application to the students transformation, He ceased public channelings. Then, in 2010 He abruptly stated it was to begin again at a Pathway gathering in England, where He announced the 'Turning of the Ages'.

Also, gathered here, are some of the promised messages from other Teachers of the Lineage, notably Mary Magdalene and Elijah.

COMING SOON

The Living Practices
The Alchemy of Living from The True Heart

Well beyond the *Christ Mind Trilogy*, Jeshua –over a several year period – revealed the profound methods of healing the roots of Separation while cultivating the ground of mystical consciousness, and restored His original teachings utilized by the Essenes, as given in the Beatitudes and Lords Prayer. Principally, these are LovesBreath and Radical Inquiry. Here, find a rich and practical treasure trove of genuine transformative practices meant to also be utterly practical in our daily lives.

COMING SOON

The Christ Mind Trilogy
Spanish Edition

The Christ Mind Trilogy in 3 volumes will be published in Spanish and we are anticipating a 4th quarter release date. Keep an eye out at WayofMasteryBooks.Com for updated release dates on all our upcoming additions.

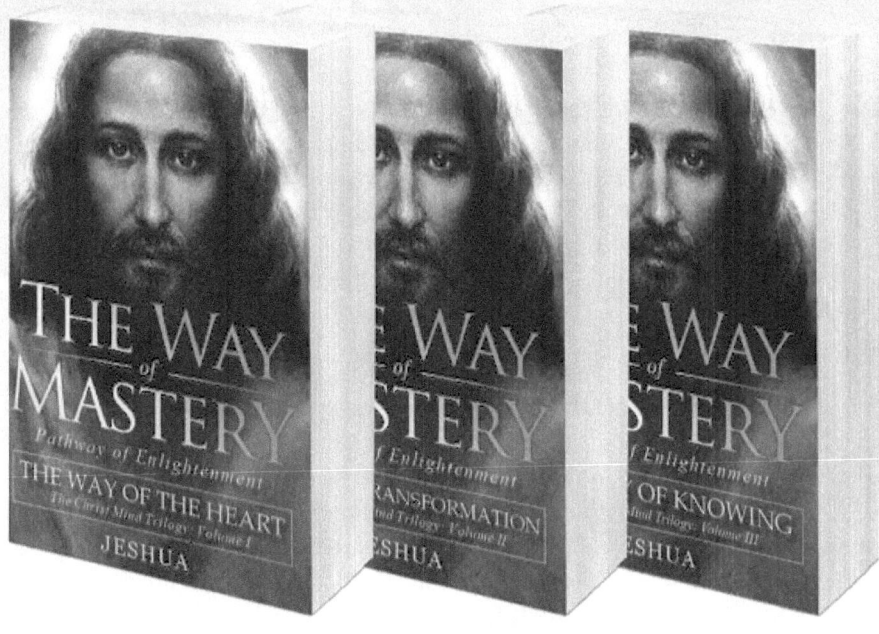

COMPLIMENTARY READING

The Essene Gospel of Peace

For the first time the complete 4 books of the Essene Gospel of Peace are available in one volume.

- *The Essene Gospel of Peace*
- *The Unknown Book of the Essenes*
- *Lost Scrolls of the Essene Brotherhood*
- *The Teachings of the Elect.*

The Essene Gospel of Peace were found in the Vatican Library and translated by Edmond Bordeaux Szekely

Edmond Bordeaux Szekely, grandson of Alexandre Szekely, eminent poet and Unitarian Bishop of Cluj, is a descendant of Csoma de Koros, Transylvanian traveler and philologist who, over 150 years ago, compiled the first grammar of the Tibetan language, the first English-Tibetan dictionary, and wrote his unsurpassed work, Asiatic Researches. He was also Librarian to the Royal Asiatic Society in India. Dr. Bordeaux earned his Ph. D. degree from the University of Paris, and other degrees from the Universities of Vienna and Leipzig. He also held professorships of Philosophy and Experimental Psychology at the University of Cluj. A well-known philologist in Sanscrit, Aramaic, Greek and Latin, Dr. Bordeaux spoke ten modern languages.

In 1928, he founded the International Biogenic Society with Nobel Prize-winning author, Romain Rolland. His most important translations, in addition to selected texts from the Dead Sea Scrolls and the Essene Gospel of Peace over a million copies in 26 languages are selected texts from the Zend Avesta and from pre Columbian codices of ancient Mexico. His last works on the Essene Way of Biogenic Living have attracted worldwide interest. He is the author of more than 80 books published in many countries on philosophy and ancient cultures.

ISBN 978-1-941489-40-6 • *308 pages, Paperback*

www.ingramcontent.com/pod-product-compliance
Lightning Source LLC
Chambersburg PA
CBHW020049170426
43199CB00009B/217